Luke

To All Nations

Thus it is written, that the Christ should suffer and on the third day rise from the dead, and that repentance and forgiveness of sins should be proclaimed in His name to all nations, beginning from Jerusalem.

Luke 24:46–47

Revised from material by
J. M. Weidenschilling

Contributions by Robert C. Baker

CONCORDIA PUBLISHING HOUSE · SAINT LOUIS

3558 S. Jefferson Ave., St. Louis, MO 63118-3968
1-800-325-3040 • cph.org

Revised from material by J. M. Weidenschilling

Edited by Robert C. Baker

This publication may be available in braille, in large print, or on cassette tape for the visually impaired. Please allow 8 to 12 weeks for delivery. Write to the Library for the Blind, 7550 Watson Rd., St. Louis, MO 63119-4409; call toll-free 1-888-215-2455; or visit the Web site: www.blindmission.org.

Manufactured in the United States of America

10 11 12 13 14 15 31 30 29 28 27 26 25

Contents

History	*Date (BC/AD)*	*Luke*
Jesus' birth in Bethlehem	ca. 6 BC	
Jesus visits the temple	AD 6	
Jesus' Baptism by John	AD 27	
Jesus' crucifixion, resurrection, and ascension	30	
Descent of the Holy Spirit in Jerusalem	30	
Martyrdom of Stephen and Paul's conversion	32	
Caligula Roman emperor	37–41	
Claudius Roman emperor	41–54	
Jerusalem Council	49/50	After council, Luke travels with Paul (Acts 16:10; see Colossians 4:14; 2 Timothy 4:11; Philemon 24)
Nero Roman emperor	54–68	
Paul imprisoned in Rome	59–63	AD 63 early date for Luke writing his Gospel; Acts written thereafter
Peter crucified upside down and Paul beheaded in Rome	67–68	
Jerusalem captured and temple destroyed	70	
	75–85	Late dates for Luke writing his Gospel; Acts written thereafter

An Outline of Luke

Following the introductory material contained in the prologue, the narratives of John's and Jesus' births, and Jesus' preparation for ministry, the Gospel of Luke contains four sections centering on Jesus' healing and teaching in Galilee, Judea, Perea, and Jerusalem. Luke is unique in that he devotes a significant amount of material to Jesus' discourses in Judea and Galilee. Luke closes his careful recording of Jesus' ministry with the Passion, resurrection, and ascension narratives. He picks up with additional events and discourses of the ascension in his second book, Acts (1:1–11).

I. Prologue (1:1–4)
II. The Births of John and Jesus (1:5–2:52)
III. Jesus' Preparation for Ministry (3:1–4:13)
IV. Jesus' Ministry in Galilee (4:14–9:50)
V. Jesus' Ministry in Judea (9:51–13:21)
VI. Jesus' Ministry in Perea (13:22–19:28)
VII. Jesus' Ministry in Jerusalem (19:29–21:38)
VIII. The Passion Narrative (21:1–23:56a)
IX. The Resurrection Narrative (23:56b–24:49)
X. The Ascension Narrative (24:50–53)

Introduction

Luke's Gospel is a Christological narrative, that is, a careful history of Jesus' life, death, resurrection, and ascension. But Luke's history, and Jesus' story, does not end with Jesus rising above the clouds. Prior to ascending into heaven, Jesus opened the minds of the apostles so that they could understand the Scriptures. He then commissioned them to preach the Good News about Him to all the nations (Luke 24:45–47). Thus, Christ's work continues as He applies the benefits of His life, death, and resurrection—through His Word and Sacraments—personally and individually through the ministry of His Church.

Liturgically, the Church literally sings the Gospel of Luke through the Magnificat (1:46–55), the Benedictus (1:68–79), the Gloria in Excelsis (2:14), the Nunc Dimittis (2:29–32), and a portion of the Sanctus ("Blessed is He who comes in the name of the Lord"; 19:38). The Church baptizes in the triune name (3:21–22), confesses her faith in her Savior (9:20), prays the Lord's Prayer (11:2–4), and eats and drinks Christ's body and blood (22:19–20). Luke is indeed a narrative about Christ, but it is even more. Through His means of grace within the Church's worship, Christ includes our story into His own.

Lesson 1

The Most Wonderful Child

Read Luke 1:1–4.

The birth or adoption of a child is a joyous occasion. In the first few verses of his Gospel, Luke describes his efforts to clearly record the joyful Christian message, which begins with the birth of two children: John the Baptist and Jesus the Christ.

1. What do you note about Luke's purpose for writing his Gospel? For whom was Luke's Gospel written?

Zechariah and Elizabeth

Before beginning his story about Jesus, Luke tells us some important things about the Savior's forerunner (Malachi 3:1; 4:5–6), John the Baptist. God chose a godly couple, Zechariah and Elizabeth, to be John's parents.

Read Luke 1:5–17.

2. How did Old Testament believers feel when they had no children (see Genesis 16:1–5; 30:1; 1 Samuel 1:5, 6; Psalm 127:3)?

3. What does this incident teach about God's answers to our prayers?

Taking God at His Word

Zechariah should have rejoiced because of the good news. Instead of believing God's Word, he followed his reason. The angel rebuked Zechariah and gave him a sign: he would lose his speech temporarily. Zechariah repented of his sin and with a stronger faith waited patiently for God to fulfill His Word.

Read verses 18–25.

4. Why is it a sin to reject God's Word when it does not agree with our human reason (see 1 Corinthians 2:9, 14)?

5. Why should we not doubt what is revealed in the Bible? How can we overcome such doubts (see John 1:46)?

The Annunciation and Magnificat

God chose Mary to be the virgin mother of the Messiah. Her Son would be the "Son of the Highest," that is, true God. Mary could not understand the mystery of her Son's birth (incarnation), but she believed God's Word and humbly submitted to His will. Her song of praise is called the Magnificat (Latin translation of the introduction).

Read verses 26–56.

6. How does the Bible prove that Jesus was born of a virgin (see Isaiah 7:14; Matthew 1:18–25)? What did this mean for Jesus' conception and birth (2 Corinthians 5:21; Hebrews 7:26–27)?

7. How is the Virgin Mary an example for all Christians?

The Forerunner's Birth

The birth of John caused great joy and wonder. Clearly God chose this child for a special purpose and work. God kept His promise: Zechariah recovered his power of speech, and his first words were a hymn called the Benedictus (Latin translation of the opening).

Read verses 57–80.

8. Explain "horn of salvation" (v. 69; see Psalm 18:2; 1 Kings 22:11). Explain "sunrise" (v. 78; see Malachi 4:2; Revelation 22:16).

9. How did Zechariah describe the people who have no knowledge of the Savior (v. 79)? What is the only way their sad condition can be changed (Isaiah 60:1–3)?

The Birth of the Christ Child

Luke's Christmas story is familiar and dear to all Christians. It is also the turning point in the world's history. Caesar Augustus, the mighty ruler of the Roman Empire, unknowingly helped carry out God's plan that the Savior should be born in Bethlehem (Micah 5:2). Only a few lowly shepherds heard the wonderful message of the Savior's birth preached by an angel (Luke 2:8–11).

Read Luke 2:1–14.

10. Why was Jesus born at Bethlehem (Matthew 2:5–6)? What does this fact prove about the Bible (Micah 5:2)?

11. Why was Jesus born in such humble circumstances (2 Corinthians 8:9)? Why did the angel call his message "good news of great joy" (Luke 2:10)?

The Shepherds at the Manger

The shepherds were some of the believing Israelites who waited in hope for the Messiah's coming. The angel's message awakened a desire to see and worship the holy child. The shepherds laid aside their earthly tasks for a while and hurried to the place where they would find their Savior. Later, they shared the good news of the Messiah's birth with others and returned to their daily tasks thanking and praising God.

Read Luke 2:15–20.

12. Where can Christ be found today? Why do many people not find Him (see Romans 10:5–21)?

13. Why do we take every opportunity to tell others about Jesus?

Simeon and Anna

Forty days after His birth, Jesus was taken to Jerusalem to be presented to the Lord in the temple (see Leviticus 12). Simeon and Anna longed for the coming of the Messiah. Simeon took the Christ Child into his arms and praised God in a hymn known as the Nunc Dimittis (Luke 2:29–32). The prophetess Anna likewise spoke to others about this child (v. 38).

Read Luke 2:22–38.

14. To redeem mankind, Christ put Himself under God's Law to fulfill it (Galatians 4:4–5). What requirements of the Law did Jesus fulfill according to Luke 2:21–24?

15. How is the Nunc Dimittis (vv. 29–32) used in church services? What does it express?

The Child Jesus

God revealed only one incident about Jesus' childhood. At the age when many children today are prepared for confirmation, Jesus studied the Holy Scriptures. Even as a boy, He faithfully applied God's Word.

Read Luke 2:40–52.

16. At twelve, a Jewish boy assumed full responsibility for his spiritual life. How does this parallel confirmation? Why is confirmation not the end of our religious training?

17. What were the first recorded words of Jesus? What did He mean by them?

In Closing

Encourage participants to begin the following activities:

- Add the newborns of your parish to your daily prayers; ask their parents how you could be of some assistance;
- Side by side, look at Luke and the Divine Service from a Lutheran hymnal to see how this Gospel is "sung";
- Read Luke 3:1–5:11 to prepare for the next lesson.

Close with prayer.

Lesson 2

Galilean Ministry

The Forerunner at Work

Read Luke 3:1–20.

The sudden appearance of a strangely dressed man at the river Jordan attracted the attention and interest of the people. Forming large crowds, they went to hear his message, hoping that he might be the Messiah. John emphatically assured them that he was not the Christ, but he informed them that the true Messiah would soon appear in their midst.

18. How was John to prepare the way for Jesus (Isaiah 40:3–5; Malachi 3:1; 4:5–6; Luke 3:4–6)?

19. Some people are offended when they are rebuked for their sins. Others say, "That was a good sermon for . . ." What effect does God's Word have on the repentant and believing sinner (vv. 8–10)?

The Holy Jesus Baptized

Read Luke 3:21–22.

John preached repentance and baptized for the remission of sins. One day, the sinless Jesus came to John to be baptized. Jesus did not need Baptism for Himself, but He submitted to Baptism as our Substitute and Savior (John 1:29; Matthew 3:15). Jesus' Baptism was simultaneously His public inauguration into the threefold office of Prophet, Priest, and King, and His anointing by the Holy Spirit for His work as the Messiah. Through our Baptism, we have become children of the triune God (Galatians 3:26–27; Romans 6:4).

20. How does the Baptism of Jesus show that there are three persons in the Holy Trinity? How does our Baptism bring us into a saving relationship with the triune God?

21. Why should a Christian frequently remind himself or herself of Christ's Baptism? of his or her own Baptism (see Matthew 3:15; Romans 6:4; Galatians 3:26–27)?

Jesus Shows How to Overcome Temptation

Read Luke 4:1–13.

Through the fall of Adam and Eve, all people came into the power of the devil and were held in bondage by him (Romans 5:12, 19; Hebrews 2:14–15). To redeem them, Christ had to submit to temptation and resist and overcome Satan, the enemy of God and man. For forty days, He permitted the devil to assail Him with temptations. But He steadfastly resisted and defeated Satan by using God's Word (see Ephesians 6:17). God's Word alone decided for Jesus what was right for Him to do. He knew and applied the Scriptures, showing us how we can overcome all temptations as well.

22. Contrast the temptation of Eve (Genesis 3) with that of Christ. Why was Satan able to lead Eve (and Adam) into sin? Why did Satan fail when he tempted Jesus?

23. Satan still tempts people to fall into the very sins with which he tempted Jesus (see 1 John 2:15–17; 1 Timothy 6:9; Genesis 3:1). How does knowing the Bible help us to overcome temptations?

Jesus' Visit in Nazareth

Read Luke 4:14–30.

In His hometown of Nazareth, Jesus worshiped in the synagogue as He had done for many years. The people had heard of His preaching and miracles in other places (v. 14). Now they also had an opportunity to hear Him for themselves. Jesus read the messianic prophecy in Isaiah 61:1–3 and declared that it was fulfilled in Him, that is, that He is the Messiah. At first, the people were amazed, but they became angry when they understood His messianic claims. He rebuked them for their unbelief by reminding them of two believing Gentiles in the Old Testament. The Savior left unbelieving Nazareth and perhaps never returned to it.

24. How is the work of the Messiah described in verses 18–19? What are some of the evil effects of sin? Compare this text with Isaiah 61:1–3.

25. How did the widow of Zarephath recognize Elijah as God's prophet (1 Kings 17:9–24)? How did Naaman prove he had become a believer (2 Kings 5:1–19)? What truth did Jesus illustrate by referring to these two stories?

Jesus, the Healer and Preacher

Read Luke 4:31–44.

For about a year and a half, Capernaum was the home of Jesus and the center of His ministry. Here He performed many miracles. The Lord had compassion and healed people with all kinds of sicknesses and diseases, including those who were possessed by the devil (vv. 40–41). Luke, the physician, was very interested in Jesus' healing miracles. The miracles prepared the people for the preaching of the Gospel, which was more important (vv. 43–44).

26. The word *synagogue* or *synagogues* appears seven times in this chapter. Why is the preaching of Jesus referred to so often?

27. How does Satan still exercise control over unbelievers? By what means alone can his power be broken (1 Peter 5:8–10; Ephesians 6:16)?

A Miraculous Catch of Fish

Read Luke 5:1–11.

Jesus often met with His disciples on the shore of the Sea of Galilee. Once, such a large crowd had gathered that He was unable to speak from the shore, so He asked Peter for the use of his boat. After the sermon, Jesus miraculously provided Peter with two boatfuls of fish! Jesus also gave Peter an unusual promise. Peter and his partners, James and John, were to give up their earthly calling and go out to catch men, that is, bring sinners into Jesus' kingdom with the net of the Gospel (see Acts 2:14, 41). The three disciples obeyed the Savior's command: "Follow Me!"

28. Peter let Jesus use his boat as a pulpit to preach the Gospel. How did other believers help Jesus (see Luke 19:28–35; John 19:38–40)?

29. When can we be certain that our labors please God? Why should we not become discouraged when we do not see immediate results (1 Corinthians 15:58)?

In Closing

Encourage participants to begin the following activities:

- If you don't do so already, (1) remind yourself of your Baptism by daily confessing your sins to God and drawing to mind Bible promises of God's forgiveness; (2) when listening to sermons, apply specific Law and Gospel statements to your own life; and (3) begin memorizing Bible passages to aid you during your times of temptation;
- Read Luke 5:12–7:10 to prepare for the next lesson.

Close with prayer.

Lesson 3

Jesus, the Messiah

Jesus Heals a Leper

Read Luke 5:12–15.

Leprosy is a horrible disease and in Bible times was incurable. Leprosy was considered highly contagious, and lepers were not permitted to mingle with other people. Nevertheless, many lepers learned that Jesus had the power to cure their disease. Luke tells us of a leper who realized that Jesus was the almighty God.

30. Mention other examples of lepers who were cured (see 2 Kings 5; Luke 17:11–19). Why do we speak of sin as spiritual leprosy? How are we cleansed from it?

31. Why did Jesus send the healed leper to the priest (see Leviticus 14)? What does God expect of us after He has bestowed material blessings upon us?

Jesus Cares for Soul and Body

Read Luke 5:17–26.

Four friends carried a paralyzed man to a house where Jesus was teaching so that He could heal him. Because of the crowd, they could not get in. Some Pharisees and scribes were also present. The friends took the man up the outside stairway to the flat roof. Then they uncovered part of the roof and lowered their friend directly in front of

Jesus. Instead of healing the man at once, Jesus first removed the cause of all evil—sin—and then brought the paralyzed man into a right relationship with God.

32. Why is forgiveness of sins more important than anything else? How does Jesus assure us that our sins are forgiven?

33. What did Jesus prove by this miracle? What effect did it have on the people and the paralytic?

The Call of Levi

Read Luke 5:27–39.

Levi, also known as Matthew, was a publican in Capernaum. Publicans collected taxes for the Roman government and were hated by the Jews. One day, Jesus passed Levi's customs house and said to him, "Follow Me." Later, at a farewell feast Levi arranged in honor of his Savior, the proud Pharisees demonstrated that Jesus offended them by associating with such outcasts of society.

34. What service did Levi, as Matthew, later render to the Church?

35. What reason do believers have to be joyful and happy (see Romans 5:1; Philippians 4:4)?

Jesus, Lord of the Sabbath

Read Luke 6:1–11.

Some people are quick to criticize. The unbelieving Jews kept a watchful eye on the Lord, and when they saw His disciples picking a few kernels of grain or observed Him healing a sick man on the Sabbath, they accused Him of breaking the Law. Jesus defended Himself and His disciples by reminding them that David ate the temple showbread as a matter of necessity (1 Samuel 21:6). He is the Son of God and therefore the "Lord of the Sabbath."

36. Why did David not commit a sin when he ate the showbread (Leviticus 24:5–9; 18:5; 1 Samuel 21:6)? How do we sin by neglecting to do a necessary good deed (see Luke 16:20–25)?

37. What miracle did Jesus perform on a Sabbath? What effect did this have on the Pharisees (v. 11)? What lesson do we learn from Jesus in this incident?

The Calling of the Apostles

Read Luke 6:12–16.

Jesus spent an entire night in prayer before He commissioned twelve of His disciples to be His apostles, His disciples in a special sense. He wished to give them further instruction in His Word and thus prepare and train them to preach the Gospel in all the world.

38. Compare the list in Luke 6:14–16 with Acts 1:13. Who does not appear in the later list? Why? What man was chosen later as the twelfth apostle (Acts 1:26)? What great apostle, called later, was not one of the Twelve (Acts 9:1–15)?

39. The apostles were the first ministers in the Church. How does Christ choose His ministers today?

The Sermon on the Mount

Read Luke 6:17–26.

Jesus preached the Sermon on the Mount to a large gathering of disciples. Luke gives us a short summary of this address. Jesus began by describing the blessings and the glory that are granted to all who believe in Him. These statements are called the Beatitudes. In the eyes of the world, Christians lack many things. However, as members of God's kingdom, they are truly blessed and happy.

40. Compare the Beatitudes in Luke 6:20–23 with those in Matthew 5:3–12. How many more are there in Matthew? How are the believers described in these additional statements?

41. Why is the ungodly world not able to understand the joy and blessedness of believers (see 1 Corinthians 2:14)?

Jesus Explains the Law of His Kingdom

Read Luke 6:27–42.

The keynote of the Sermon on the Plain is the love that flows from true faith in Christ. The believer loves his or her neighbor and desires the temporal and spiritual welfare of all people, regardless of who they are. The believer also loves his or her enemies, befriends them, and even prays for his or her persecutors.

42. How does the Golden Rule found in Luke 6:31 (also Matthew 7:12) require much more than avoiding sinful deeds? Why does Jesus place the emphasis on "do" rather than on "Thou shalt not"?

43. Why can unbelievers not fulfill the requirements of the Sermon on the Mount? Why do believers strive to fulfill them (v. 36; see also 1 John 4:19, 21)?

Jesus Recognizes His Disciples

Read Luke 6:43–7:10.

Jesus divides all people into two groups: believers and unbelievers. Believers, whose hearts have been cleansed and regenerated by the Gospel, are like good fruit-bearing trees. They build upon the solid rock: Christ in His Word and grace.

Unbelievers are like worthless trees. They build only for this life, putting their trust and hope in their own righteousness.

44. What is the foundation on which Christians rest their hope? What is all other ground called?

45. What did the Jews praise about the centurion? What did Jesus praise? Why are both statements important (see Luke 7:4–5, 9)?

In Closing

Encourage participants to begin the following activities:

- Inquire how you might offer assistance in a healing ministry either in your congregation or in your community;
- Resolve to bear your cross, whatever it may be, with peace and determination, relying on the Lord's help;
- Read Luke 7:11–8:56 to prepare for the next lesson.

Close with prayer.

Lesson 4

The Compassionate Savior

Jesus Comforts the Bereaved

Read Luke 7:11–17.

Traveling southwest from Capernaum, Jesus and His disciples came to Nain. The only son of a widowed, grief-stricken mother was being carried in a funeral procession to his last resting place. The procession halted when Jesus stepped up and touched the bier. Comforting the mother He said, "Do not weep." He then spoke to the dead son, restored him to life, and gave him back to his mother. All who witnessed the miracle were filled with awe and praised God.

46. What special comfort can we give Christians who mourn over the death of loved ones (see John 11:25–26; 1 Thessalonians 4:13–17)?

47. How does this story illustrate the comforting doctrine of the resurrection?

The Messengers from John

Read Luke 7:18–23.

John the Baptist was a prisoner in Herod's castle at Machaerus, near the Dead Sea (see 3:19–20). The forerunner could no longer serve his Master in the public ministry. Some of his disciples had already joined Jesus (see John 1:35–37; 3:30). John was grieved that some of them still clung to him instead of following Christ. He knew that Jesus was the promised Messiah, and he wanted his disciples to become convinced of this truth. Jesus proved by His miracles that He is the Son of God and the Savior of the world. Those who accept the testimony of His Word in true faith, Jesus calls blessed (Luke 6:23; see 2:34).

48. Why is it unlikely that John doubted the Messiahship of Jesus (see John 1:29–34; 3:28–32; Luke 7:24–27)?

49. What advice would you give to people who express doubts about Jesus being the Son of God and the world's Savior (John 5:39; 1:45, 49)?

Jesus' Testimony about John

Read Luke 7:24–35.

After John's disciples departed, Jesus gave public testimony to John. Christ plainly says that John was His forerunner and places him above all the prophets. However, the least believer of the New Testament is greater than John because John saw only the beginning of Christ's work. He did not see the full light of the Gospel that we see recorded in the New Testament.

50. What advantages do we Christians have over the Old Testament prophets? over John the Baptist (see 1 Peter 1:10–12)?

51. What does Jesus say about those who refuse to believe the message of His ministers (Luke 10:16; 2 Corinthians 5:20)?

In the House of Simon the Pharisee

Read Luke 7:36–50.

Jesus wants to save all people (John 17:1–3). For that reason He accepted an invitation to a Pharisee's house. But this proud man did not care for a Savior; he did not even show common courtesy to his guest. In contrast, a woman of the city known for her sinful life quietly stole into the Pharisee's house and bent over the feet of Jesus, weeping bitter tears of repentance. She knew that Jesus would forgive her. By relating the parable of the two debtors, Jesus taught that all sinners need repentance and forgiveness, including the Pharisee.

52. What is the proper attitude of Christians toward the lost? How does the parable of the two debtors apply to all people today?

53. What is the meaning of verse 47? What comes first: our love or God's forgiveness (see 1 John 4:19)? What prompts God to forgive sins?

The Parable of the Sower

Read Luke 8:1–15.

Jesus speaks of the Gospel as seed that is sown into the hearts of people. Christ Himself sows this seed when ministers preach the Word or when people read the Bible (Romans 10:17). However, not everyone benefits by hearing and reading God's Word. Jesus mentions three kinds of people in whose hearts the Gospel does not produce a living and abiding faith. He then compares the hearts of the final group of hearers to good ground. These are the true believers.

54. What means did Jesus use to awaken faith in the hearts of His hearers (v. 1)? How did some women who followed Jesus give evidence of their faith (vv. 2–3)?

55. How does this parable show the hearing of God's Word having different effects on different hearers? How do you apply sermons to yourself personally?

The Parable of the Candle

Read Luke 8:16–21.

What person would be so foolish as to light a lamp and cover it up or set it where it would do no one any good? Believers have the light of the Gospel, which enlightens our hearts. We are not to hide this light. As lights, Christians are to do good works and give the Gospel to others (Isaiah 60:1; Acts 4:20; 1 Peter 2:9, 12). The hearing and doing of God's Word is so important that Jesus again emphasizes it in verse 21. Faith unites us with Jesus and with all our fellow believers.

56. Give two reasons why believers are referred to as lights (Isaiah 60:1; Matthew 5:14–16).

57. What does Jesus call all those who believe in Him (v. 21)? Why is this comforting to us? What are believers called in Ephesians 2:19 and 1 Peter 2:9–10?

The Storm on the Lake

Read Luke 8:22–25.

Some of Jesus' disciples had spent much of their lives as fishermen on the Sea of Galilee. They were familiar with the violent storms that often swept suddenly through the deep gorge of the lake. One day, they were caught in a tempest. In their desperate condition, they awoke Jesus from His sleep and implored His help. He immediately quieted the storm. Turning to His disciples, He asked,

“Where is your faith?” The Lord sometimes sends severe trials in order to reveal our weakness and to teach us to cling more firmly to our God.

58. Why did the disciples have no reason to fear, even though Jesus was asleep in the ship (see Psalm 121:3–4)? Why can we be sure of God’s help in all our troubles?

59. Which commandment condemns lack of trust in God as sin? Why is it comforting to know that the disciples sometimes had a weak faith?

The Demon-Possessed Man

Read Luke 8:26–39.

In the country of the Gerasenes, Jesus met a man who for a long time had been tortured by many devils (“legion,” a whole regiment). These evil spirits abused the body of this man. They knew that Jesus was the Son of God, and they feared His judgment. By driving out the devils, Jesus transformed the demon-possessed man. Jesus has set us, too, free from Satan’s power. All who believe in Him are delivered from the tyranny of the devil.

60. How does this passage show that the devil is the enemy of God and man? Why should we not fear Satan’s power?

61. How do some people today show the same attitude toward Jesus as did the Gerasenes? What do 1 Timothy 6:9–10 and Luke 12:20–21 say about such people?

Faith Purified by Tribulations

Read Luke 8:40–56.

The story of the sick woman and Jairus shows that the Lord allows us to suffer so that we seek Him for help. The sick woman immediately received what she desired (v. 48). However, the delay caused by her cure was a hard lesson for Jairus. His faith was severely tried when he learned that his daughter had died. However, the merciful Savior assured him that the child would be restored to him in good health. By speaking two words (Mark 5:41), Jesus brought the dead girl back to life.

62. How does the case of Jairus illustrate the power of prayer?

63. Why should a Christian not be afraid of death (see Philippians 1:21–23; Job 19:25–27)? Why did Jesus say, "She is not dead but sleeping" (v. 52)?

In Closing

Encourage participants to begin the following activities:

- Volunteer to help the bereaved in your congregation by sending a card, sharing companionship, or providing a meal;
- Let your light shine by inviting your neighbors to an informal Bible study in your home;
- Read Luke 9:1–10:37 to prepare for the next lesson.

Close with prayer.

Lesson 5

Disciples Trained for Service

The Mission of the Twelve

Read Luke 9:1–9.

Jesus Himself could not visit all parts of Galilee. In order that other areas might learn that the Messiah had come, He sent out His twelve apostles to preach, cast out demons, and heal the sick. This missionary tour was valuable training and experience for the Twelve.

64. What do you think about people who claim to have the power to work miracles? On what does the Church rely for the ultimate miracle (see Romans 10:17)?

65. What further instructions were given concerning those who preach the Gospel (see Luke 10:7; 1 Corinthians 9:14; Galatians 6:6)? What provision should be made for their support?

The Feeding of the Five Thousand

Read Luke 9:10–17.

This familiar story is recorded in all four Gospels. After the return of the Twelve, Jesus withdrew to a thinly settled district northeast of the lake, near Bethsaida Julias. A tremendous crowd followed Him. Jesus multiplied five loaves so that five thousand people had more than enough to eat. Jesus can solve all the problems of our lives. He gives us what we need, when we need it.

66. Why should we not worry or despair when the supplies for our daily needs seem scant (see Psalm 37:5, 7, 16, 29)?

67. Why do Christians pray before and after meals (v. 16)?

The Transfiguration

Read Luke 9:18–36.

When Jesus was again alone with His disciples, He asked them what the people generally thought of Him. Peter made the glorious confession that Jesus is "the Christ of God" (9:20; see Matthew 16:16). Jesus gave three of His disciples the wonderful mountaintop experience of seeing their Master in His heavenly glory.

68. Peter, James, and John immediately recognized Moses and Elijah. What does this suggest about believers in heaven (see 1 Corinthians 13:12)?

69. How does God's command to "listen to Him!" (v. 35) apply to our daily lives?

Humility and Greatness

Read Luke 9:37–50.

When Jesus came down from the mountain, He healed a sick boy who had been tortured by the devil. He severely rebuked the disciples, who had not been able to heal the boy, for lack of faith. He again foretold His Passion, but the disciples only quarreled among themselves about the places of honor they hoped to occupy in His kingdom. In Christ's kingdom, those are greatest who are most humble. To illustrate this truth, Jesus set a little child before them.

70. Why did Jesus often refer to His Passion? Why should we daily think of His suffering on the cross (see 1 Corinthians 2:2)?

71. Why can no one be neutral before Jesus and the Gospel (v. 50)?

The Right Attitude of Disciples

Read Luke 9:51–62.

Jesus made His final departure from Galilee and began His journey toward Jerusalem. When He and His disciples reached a village in Samaria, the people refused to grant Him lodging. James and John were furious at the Samaritans' unkind attitude, so much so that they asked Jesus for the power to punish these people, as Elijah had done. The Lord rebuked His two disciples for their vengeful spirit. He had not come to destroy but to save sinners. This merciful spirit of Jesus was to be the attitude of the disciples also.

72. Why was it a good thing that Jesus did not punish the inhospitable Samaritans (see Acts 8:4–8)? What lesson can we learn from this?

73. Why must all believers be willing to practice self-denial and bring sacrifices for Jesus' sake?

The Seventy Missionaries

Read Luke 10:1–16.

Because Gospel preaching was greatly needed and the time was short, Jesus sent out a second group of seventy missionaries. They were to preach the Gospel of peace to the people in Berea and Judea, which the Lord referred to as great harvest fields. He urged His disciples to pray diligently for the Father to send out more laborers into the world's mission fields.

74. How does Jesus describe the world's mission fields (Matthew 9:36–38; John 4:35–38)? Apply this to our mission opportunities today.

75. What will our prayers for missions accomplish? In which petition of the Lord's Prayer do we pray for the ingathering of souls?

The Missionaries' Report

Read Luke 10:17–24.

What the seventy missionaries experienced filled their hearts with joy. Jesus wants Christians to rejoice over the success of the Gospel. But the chief reason for their happiness should be that their names are inscribed in the Book of Life in heaven.

76. Why should the fact that our names are recorded in heaven be the chief reason for our happiness (see Philippians 4:3–4)? How does this affect our daily lives (see Revelation 3:5; 20:12; Isaiah 43:1–3)?

77. Why do many people of the world refuse to believe the Gospel (v. 21; see also 1 Corinthians 1:18–29; 2:14)? What is said of the "infants" in 1 Peter 2:2? Explain.

The Good Samaritan

Read Luke 10:25–37.

One of the best-known stories of the Bible is that of the Good Samaritan. The example of the Good Samaritan shows us what it means to "love our neighbor as ourselves." Jesus is our Good Samaritan who has saved and healed us from sin; we should, therefore, help all who are in bodily and spiritual need.

78. When does the Church act as a Good Samaritan? Mention institutions of mercy your congregation supports. How can you help in this work?

79. How did the Good Samaritan help the injured man? What lesson can we learn from this in regard to helping the needy?

In Closing

Encourage participants to begin the following activities:

- Support your pastor(s) and other church workers through prayer, affirmation, and financial giving;
- Initiate or support your parish's involvement in providing food and other forms of assistance to the community's needy;
- Read Luke 10:38–12:48 to prepare for the next lesson.

Close with prayer.

Lesson 6

Comfort and Warning

Mary and Martha

Read Luke 10:38–42.

One of the loveliest pictures we have in the Bible is that of Jesus in the home of Mary and Martha. These sisters were true disciples, and they were very happy when they could entertain Jesus as their beloved and honored guest. The Lord indeed appreciated the efforts of His friends to provide for His comfort and serve Him. But He wanted first of all to serve them with the blessings of His Gospel. After Jesus has refreshed our souls with the Gospel, He is pleased to have us honor and serve Him in the faithful performance of our earthly duties.

80. How can we have Jesus as a permanent guest in our homes? What can our home life be like when we always think of Jesus as present?

81. Why should every Christian family daily take time for family devotions? How should family members imitate Mary's example when there is opportunity to hear God's Word?

The Believers' Life of Prayer

Read Luke 11:1–13.

The disciples often saw Jesus praying to His Father. Wishing that they could pray as He did, they asked Him to teach them to pray as

John had taught his disciples. Jesus gladly granted their request by teaching them the Lord's Prayer. This model prayer includes everything that we need for our bodies and souls. Jesus does not limit our praying to this one form He has given. He wants us to pray often, to lead a life of prayer, and to make all our needs and requests known to God (see Philippians 4:6).

82. Compare Luke 11:2–4 with Matthew 6:9–13. Note the differences in the wording of the two accounts of the Lord's Prayer.

83. How does Jesus assure us (vv. 11–12) that God gives us only good gifts?

Unbelievers Ruled by Satan

Read Luke 11:14–36.

Luke again tells us about Jesus' healing a man who was possessed by a devil that had deprived him of speech. Instead of rejoicing in the miracle, the unbelieving Jews blasphemously accused Him of working with Satan. They were not satisfied with Jesus' many miracles but demanded some special sign from heaven to prove He was the Messiah. The Lord promised the Jews a sign that if rejected by them would finally condemn them. He referred to Jonah's escape from the great fish as a sign of His own resurrection. Those who reject that Jesus rose bodily from the dead will be lost.

84. Why is a person either in Christ's kingdom or in Satan's kingdom?

85. What effect did Jonah's preaching have on the Ninevites (Jonah 3:5–10)? Why is the example of the Jews a warning to indifferent Christians?

God's Judgment upon Unbelievers

Read Luke 11:37–54.

Jesus again accepted an invitation to dine with a Pharisee (see 7:36). Purposely, He omitted the customary washing before eating. The Pharisees regarded such outward matters as more important than obedience to the commandments of God. They were deeply offended when they saw that Jesus neglected this ceremony. Jesus exposed their rank hypocrisy. He also condemned the religious lawyers for perverting God's Word by their false teachings, thus preventing the people from learning the way of salvation (v. 52). These woes of divine judgment filled the hearts of His enemies with hatred.

86. Show how the Pharisees hypocritically performed certain outward acts (vv. 39–44). Is their form of piety imitated today? Explain.

87. For which sins did Jesus rebuke the lawyers (vv. 45–52)?

Warning against Hypocrisy and Disloyalty

Read Luke 12:1–12.

Hypocrisy works secretly in the heart like yeast in bread. No man can see it in action; nevertheless, it gradually gains possession of a person's whole heart and life. Hypocrites may be able to deceive people, but they cannot deceive God. On the other hand, believers should have nothing to conceal. Their lives should be like open books that all may read. Believers have no reason to be afraid of people when they confess the truth; the most human beings can do is kill the body. Knowing that we have an almighty protector, we should be willing at all times to confess Him before people as our Lord and Savior.

88. Why did Jesus often denounce the Pharisees? Why should we especially guard against hypocrisy (see Acts 5:1–11)?

89. Why should Christians continue their mealtime prayers even at public places such as restaurants? Why should they continue family devotions and attend church when they have guests in their homes?

Warning against Covetousness

Read Luke 12:13–21.

While Jesus was warning His disciples against spiritual dangers, He was interrupted by a man who had been thinking about his father's inheritance during the sermon. He foolishly believed that Jesus would help him gain an advantage over his brother. The Lord rebuked this man and used the occasion to warn all His hearers against covetousness. Greed is a dangerous vice, and it is foolish for a person to ruin his or her soul for the sake of money (see 1 Timothy 6:7).

90. Why did Jesus refuse to settle the matter of inheritance (v. 14)? What lesson did Jesus thereby wish to teach (see 20:25)?

91. Why did God call the rich man a fool? How would a believer have acted after receiving great blessings from God?

Warning against the Cares of Life

Read Luke 12:22–31.

People who set their hearts on earthly things are sure to be tortured with many cares and worries. Worry is sinful; it is a lack of trust in God. We should learn from the birds that do not worry and from the flowers that God clothes with beauty. How much more will He not provide for the well-being of our bodies and souls, which are to live with Him eternally! The believer's continual prayer is to remain a member of the heavenly kingdom, a blessed disciple of Jesus (v. 31).

92. Explain why worry is sinful. Which petition of the Lord's Prayer will help keep us from worrying? What comforting promise does Jesus give to all who seek God's kingdom (Luke 12:31; Matthew 6:33)?

93. While it is wrong to worry, is it wrong to work, to save, and to provide for the future (see Genesis 2:15; 1 Thessalonians 4:11; 2 Thessalonians 3:10)?

Comfort for the "Little Flock"

Read Luke 12:32–48.

When believers think about the Church's position in the world, they might feel dismayed. Believers are only a "little flock," like helpless sheep, surrounded by enemies. But Jesus, who is on our side, is much stronger than those who stand against us. Our heavenly Father wants to give us the imperishable treasures of heaven. We should use our worldly goods to help our needy fellow people and fix our hearts on the treasures kept securely for us in heaven. Let us therefore be faithful and wise stewards, ready to meet Jesus at His coming.

94. What does Jesus say about His flock in John 10:11–18, 27–29? Why should this assurance comfort us in the trials of life?

95. In what sense are all Christians stewards of Christ? What responsibilities do we have as stewards?

In Closing

Encourage participants to begin the following activities:

- If you do not do so already, begin a regular time of daily Bible reading and prayer for you and your family;
- To combat covetousness, in your daily prayers give thanks for salvation, health, family, friends, shelter, food, clothing, and for all of God's good and gracious gifts;
- Read Luke 12:49–14:35 to prepare for the next lesson.

Close with prayer.

Lesson 7

God's Power to Save

Opposition to the Gospel

Read Luke 12:49–59.

Jesus preached in Perea as He slowly continued His journey to Jerusalem. He clearly foresaw His Passion and death awaiting Him there. Although He was determined to become the sacrifice for the sins of the world, His human nature dreaded the thought of the cross. Nevertheless, He was anxious to complete the work of our redemption so that the Gospel of salvation could be preached to all people. Sadly, Jesus knew that some would refuse to forgive their fellow people, showing that they do not believe in God's forgiveness. Unless Jesus is our Savior today, He will become our judge on the Last Day.

96. Knowing how the very thought of His Passion filled the soul of Jesus with dread, how should we feel toward sin (see Isaiah 53:5; Hebrews 6:6)?

97. Compare verses 58–59 with Matthew 5:23–26; 6:14–15. Why should we seek to become reconciled with a brother without delay?

The Call to Repentance

Read Luke 13:1–9.

Many of the Jews believed that, because they belonged to God's Church, they did not need to repent of any sins. When they heard of the misfortunes of other people, they were certain that these persons were being punished for some great wickedness. Jesus, however, showed that all calamities in the world are a lesson of warning and an earnest call to repentance. "Except ye repent, ye shall all likewise perish." In the parable of the fig tree, Jesus shows that God is indeed merciful and often extends His season of grace.

98. Mention ways in which God is warning the world and calling people to repentance. What can Christians do after calamities such as tornadoes, hurricanes, and tsunamis?

99. What does the parable of the fig tree teach us about Jesus (Romans 8:34; 1 John 2:1–2)? How are we to apply this parable?

The Gospel Brings Deliverance

Read Luke 13:10–21.

One day as Jesus was teaching in a synagogue, He noticed a woman who had been handicapped for eighteen years. Although she was a true daughter of Abraham, a believer, God had permitted Satan to afflict the poor woman for a long time. By His Word, Jesus healed the woman from her infirmity. Most of the people present joined the healed woman in rejoicing and in praising God. This gave Jesus an opportunity to teach through two parables (see Matthew 13:31–35; Mark 4:30–32) how His Church grows and spreads in the world and how the Gospel changes sinners' hearts and lives.

100. How did the woman prove that she was a true spiritual descendant of Abraham (see Romans 4:16)? What do people lose by neglecting Word and Sacrament?

101. In what respect is the ruler of the synagogue a warning to all Christians?

The Door to Eternal Life

Read Luke 13:22–30.

Jesus admonishes all to "strive to enter through the narrow door." He is the only door to eternal life (see John 10:9; 14:6). By faith we enter the door of heaven. It is called a "narrow door" because no one can enter it loaded down with sins and self-righteousness. Only those can enter whose sins are forgiven and who appear before God in the righteousness of Christ. As long as the Gospel is preached, the door stands open. It is shut to all who die in unbelief (Hebrews 9:27). After this life, it will be too late to repent and seek admission to heaven.

102. How are people deceiving themselves by thinking that they can get to heaven without repentance and faith (Mark 16:16)?

103. How does Matthew 25:1–13 explain why some churchgoers will not gain admission to heaven? How does Luke 13:28–30 apply to them?

Jesus Grieves over Unbelievers

Read Luke 13:31–35.

Jesus came into the world to suffer and die for all sinners. He proved by His miracles that He was the Son of God, and as soon as He finished His task, He would be exalted (Philippians 2:8–11). Though people sought to destroy Him, He wanted to save them all. How much loving care the Lord had bestowed upon the Jews! Sadly, the number of those who received Him as their Messiah was small. The majority rejected Him. The Lord still grieves over those lost in unbelief. How much He has done to save us all!

104. How did the Jews try to silence an Old Testament prophet (Amos 7:10–13)? What did the apostles say when they were forbidden to preach (Acts 5:28–29)?

105. What does the picture of the hen illustrate in regard to Jesus? Why is this very comforting to us (see Ezekiel 33:11; 1 Timothy 2:4; 2 Peter 3:9)?

A Lesson on Humility and Charity

Read Luke 14:1–14.

In a Pharisee's house, Jesus not only healed a man afflicted with dropsy but also gave His enemies another lesson as to the true meaning and observance of the Sabbath. What Jesus had to say to His host is an important lesson for us also. God does not object that we enjoy dinners and sociability with our friends. However, He will hold us accountable if we are concerned only with our personal enjoyment and neglect to show true Christian love to the poor and afflicted (see 16:19–31; Matthew 25:41–46). God will mercifully reward all deeds of love that flow from faith.

106. When is taking the lowest seat not a sign of humility? What example of true humility does Paul give us in Philippians 2:5–11?

107. Explain the meaning of verses 13–14. Show how a believer acts in accordance with this admonition.

Parable of the Great Supper

Read Luke 14:15–24.

While Jesus was a guest in the house of a sinner, He extended the invitation to all people to attend the feast in His house: "Come, for everything is now ready" (v. 17). God has prepared salvation for all people, and He offers all the blessings of His grace to us. The Gospel is His invitation to the heavenly feast. The proud Pharisees rejected the Gospel, but many despised publicans, sinners, and humble fishermen became Jesus' disciples. "Still there is room" (v. 22)—God wants more guests. Since Pentecost, the Lord has been sending His disciples into the whole world to preach the Gospel (see Matthew 28:18–20; Mark 16:15; Acts 1:8).

108. How does the parable prove that we cannot earn salvation by our own deeds? Show that the Gospel makes no distinction among people.

109. What encouragement does Christ give us in the parable of the great supper to take an active part in evangelism and mission work (see 1 Corinthians 15:58)?

Continuance in God's House

Read Luke 14:25–35.

Only through faith in Christ do we become members of His kingdom. But if we would remain His disciples, we must grow in sanctification and be willing to offer the sacrifices Jesus requires of His followers (see 9:23–26; Matthew 10:37–38). If we truly love our Savior, we will give Him our whole heart, and no sacrifice for His sake will be too great for us. We must also accept the cross He lays upon us and bear it patiently for His sake. We must keep our eyes fixed upon the heavenly life and shun no cost in the service of our Lord.

110. How do churchgoers imitate the example of the foolish builder and the unwise king? What does it mean that we should "count the cost"?

111. When does a Christian act like good salt? How does one become saltless?

In Closing

Encourage participants to begin the following activities:

- Locate and greet first-time visitors to your congregation after the worship service;
- Support the Church's care for disaster victims through prayer, financial gifts, and volunteering;
- Read Luke 15:1–16:31 to prepare for the next lesson.

Close with prayer.

Lesson 8

"Jesus Sinners Doth Receive"

Joy over Finding the Lost

Read Luke 15:1–10.

Jesus' personality and preaching attracted people. Several times we are told that "the tax collectors and sinners were all drawing near to hear Him." The self-righteous Pharisees and scribes who saw this scornfully exclaimed, "This man receives sinners and eats with them." The title "friend of tax collectors and sinners" (Luke 7:34)—was meant to ridicule Jesus. He gladly accepted the title, which expressed the purpose of His coming into the world. The parables of the lost sheep and the lost coin clearly show God's desire for every person to be saved.

112. What does the parable of the lost sheep teach us in regard to ourselves? in regard to Jesus? (See Isaiah 53:6; 1 Peter 2:25; and John 10:16.)

113. How is the woman in the second parable a type of the Church? of the individual believer?

Pardon for Penitent Sinners

Read Luke 15:11–24.

The story of the prodigal son may be the most beautiful parable in the Bible; indeed, there is nothing more beautiful than the kindness and joy with which the father welcomed his returning son. Before the young man could finish his confession, he knew that all his sins were forgiven. The loving father had taken his ragged and degraded boy affectionately into his arms. The dark record of the past was all forgotten. The penitent sinner was restored to all the honors and privileges of a son. This, the climax of the parable, portrays the love of God and the joyful welcome the sinner receives when he or she becomes a believer.

114. How does the parable prove that "the way of the treacherous is their ruin"? What effect does sin have on the body? on the soul?

115. How does the parable show that salvation is only by God's grace?

Lost in the Father's House

Read Luke 15:25–32.

Our chapter really contains the story of two lost sons. The elder son, indeed, had never left his father's house. Nevertheless, he proved by his conduct that he had excluded himself from the joyful festivities of his father's house. He represents the self-righteous Pharisees, who were displeased with God's grace for sinners. This son heartily despised the younger son, whom he would not even acknowledge as a brother. The joyful celebration over the return of his lost brother grated on his ears. Patiently and kindly, the father tried to win also this lost son. Did he succeed? We do not know.

116. Why is the story of the elder son a warning example for every churchgoer?

117. Mention several sins that the elder brother committed. How do self-righteous people prove that they, too, are sinners?

For Further Study and Discussion

118. Find a painting of the Good Shepherd and describe it. Why do we love to think of Jesus as our Good Shepherd (see Psalm 23; Ezekiel 34:11–24; John 10:11–16)?

119. What responsibility does the Church have toward members who fall away?

Giving an Account

Read Luke 16:1–12.

The Bible has much to say about God's grace and Christ's love for sinners. However, we should not believe that how we live in this world is irrelevant. Our earthly life is to be spent preparing for eternity. We are God's stewards over our earthly possessions, which include our time, talents, and property. God will bless a faithful steward by placing him or her over more of His earthly treasures. On the Last Day, all whom we help on earth will testify to our deeds of love as fruits of our faith.

120. Why can't we do what we please with our earthly possessions? How does God often show that all things belong to Him?

121. When are we faithful stewards of our time, talents, and property? How does the parable solve the problem of giving to the Church?

Serving Two Masters

Read Luke 16:13–18.

The stewardship of money is a great privilege and, when rightly used, will result in rich blessings. But there is also a great danger connected with the possession of wealth. A selfish and sinful use of it makes one a slave of an idol and thus a servant of Satan. People have always tried to serve both God and money. Such were the Pharisees; people like them are found in the Church. However, love of money closes the heart against God's love. The Pharisees gave ample evidence that they were not serving God.

122. Why can a person who is ruled by love of money not serve God (see 1 Timothy 6:9–10)?

123. How might we try to serve both God and money? What may be the result? How can we prevent money from ruling over us?

A Man Who Had No Friend in Eternity

Read Luke 16:19–31.

One of the most earnest warnings in the Bible is the parable of the rich man and Lazarus. It is the story of one man who served money and of another who served God. The surplus or lack of wealth had nothing to do with their fate in eternity, for both poor Lazarus and rich Abraham are in heaven. In unbelief, the rich man failed to recognize his obligations of stewardship on earth. With his money, he made no friends for eternity and lived only for himself and for this world. On the other hand, Lazarus trusted in God, as his name ("God is help") implies and as his presence in heaven shows.

124. How is the rich man a warning to people who enjoy prosperity in this life? Why did Abraham, who had been rich, get to heaven?

125. Why is it foolish to deny that there is a hell? What does our text tell us about the place of the damned (see Isaiah 66:24; Mark 9:43–48)?

In Closing

Encourage participants to begin the following activities:

- Ask your pastor how you may help in your congregation's evangelism efforts to the community;
- Resolve to increase your current level of financial giving to your congregation, Synod, and mission organizations;
- Read Luke 17:1–18:43 to prepare for the next lesson.

Close with prayer.

Lesson 9

Disciples Pray for Increase of Faith

Lord, "Increase Our Faith!"

Read Luke 17:1–10.

The apostles realized that they needed a strong faith and a great deal of love. To fulfill this important duty, we should do as they did: pray for an increase of faith. A strong faith is one of the greatest assets in our lives. Jesus shows how faith enables us to overcome all ill feeling toward other people and to serve the Lord with godly lives. Our good works are the fruits of faith. God delights in them and will graciously reward us for them. But we must never think that we merit eternal life by our faithfulness to God.

126. What do we reveal about ourselves when we refuse to forgive someone who has sinned against us (see Matthew 18:35; James 2:13)?

127. Why is it good sincerely to confess that we are unworthy servants of God? What does it mean when God must call us that (Matthew 25:30)?

The Missing Nine

Read Luke 17:11–19.

We feel hurt when someone repays our kindness with ingratitude. The story of the ten lepers shows us that the Lord is also grieved when people neglect to thank Him for His blessings. After their healing, nine of the lepers gave no further thought to Jesus. But one, a Samaritan, realized what a great blessing Jesus had bestowed upon him. He immediately returned and thanked his benefactor, worshiping Him as his God and Savior. How happy he must have felt when he saw how pleased Jesus was with the expressions of his grateful heart!

128. Why is adversity a greater blessing for some people than prosperity? What can be said of people who call on God only when in trouble?

129. What does ingratitude toward God evidence? Why should a Christian thank God every day (see explanation of the First Article of the Creed)?

A Dangerous World

Read Luke 17:20–37.

The Pharisees ridiculed Jesus' preaching about the kingdom of God. Unbelief blinded them from seeing that He was the Messiah. The ungodly world ridicules Christianity and taunts believers because of their faith (see 2 Peter 3:3–5). However, we have something that sustains us in all trials of life and keeps us in the true faith: the Gospel that reminds us of Jesus' sufferings on our behalf (v. 25). Remembering what Jesus has done for us makes it easier to bear our crosses. The Gospel fills our hearts with the hope of eternal glory.

130. How can we recognize the presence of Christ's kingdom of grace (Isaiah 55:11)? How can we know whether we are in this kingdom?

131. Why does Jesus want us to "remember Lot's wife" (see Genesis 19:26)? How do some imitate her conduct today? What are the results?

The Right Kind of Prayer

Read Luke 18:1–14.

In the parable of the persistent widow, Jesus shows how we should pray and what we can accomplish by our prayers. God will answer the persevering prayers of His children who cry to Him day and night! The parable of the Pharisee and the tax collector shows that when a person boasts of moral goodness and splendid accomplishments, this is not praying to God. By these two parables, Jesus teaches that faith continues in prayer despite severe trials and disappointments and that faith-filled prayer is offered in a spirit of deep humility.

132. Compare verses 1–8 with Luke 11:5–8 and Genesis 32:24–30. What do these passages teach us about prayers that bring results?

133. How did St. Paul imitate the example of the tax collector (1 Timothy 1:15)? What does this parable teach regarding the spirit in which we should pray?

Jesus Loves Children and Youth

Read Luke 18:15–23.

The Bible presents a beautiful picture when it tells us about parents bringing their babies to Jesus to have Him bless them! The disciples showed a mistaken zeal and had a wrong conception of Christ's work when they looked upon the efforts of these mothers as an unwelcome disturbance. Jesus wants infants and children to be brought to Him in Holy Baptism. He blesses them by working faith in their hearts and making them members of His kingdom. But Jesus also wants to be the Savior and Friend of young people as well.

134. Mention ways in which parents become guilty of keeping their children from Jesus. Why should infants and children be baptized?

135. How is the rich ruler an example to young people? a warning? Would he have been saved by giving his riches to the poor? Explain.

A Profitable Exchange

Read Luke 18:24–43.

Jesus was painfully disappointed in the choice made by the young ruler (v. 24). This incident moved Him to show how, without God's help, a change of heart is impossible. Jesus said that His followers would be rewarded for their service, but it would be a reward of grace, which they would begin to enjoy already in this life (vv. 29–30). By reminding them again of His Passion (vv. 31–33), He showed that He would sacrifice much more for their sake than He asks of His followers (2 Corinthians 8:9). In Jericho, Jesus healed a blind beggar who recognized and acknowledged Him as the Messiah. Faith had given the blind man the power to find his Savior.

136. What does the apostle say about riches in 1 Timothy 6:9–10? Show that a poor person can trust in riches just as easily as a rich person (see Mark 10:24–25)?

137. Why should we not regret any sacrifices we make for Christ and His Church (2 Corinthians 8:9)?

In Closing

Encourage participants to begin the following activities:

- As part of your daily devotions, begin reading the Book of Concord, starting with the creeds;
- Ask how you might support the children's or youth ministry at your congregation or in your community;
- Read Luke 19:1–20:47 to prepare for the next lesson.

Close with prayer.

Lesson 10

The King Seeks Subjects

A Businessman Who Became a Christian

Read Luke 19:1–10.

Zacchaeus was in charge of the customs station, a business that had enriched him considerably. But this tax collector's conscience finally began to trouble him. When Jesus kindly looked up at him perched in a tree, Zacchaeus's life began to change! The salvation and peace that Jesus brought filled Zacchaeus's heart with joy and with the desire to live a godly life, beginning by making amends.

138. How did Zacchaeus prove that he was sincere in seeking peace for his soul?

139. Why did Jesus not demand that Zacchaeus give up his wealth? In what way do we follow Zacchaeus's example?

Until I Come Back!

Read Luke 19:11–27.

Jesus was on the way to Jerusalem, where His disciples hoped He would set up an earthly kingdom. To correct their false ideas, Jesus told the parable of the minas, showing that His kingdom would appear visibly and in glory only when He returned on the Last Day. The Gospel is the "mina," or coin, with which Christians are to do business in the world. On Judgment Day, Christ will return, and all Christians will have to render an account to Him of how they made use of His Word.

140. Why is Jesus especially concerned about the use we make of the Gospel?

141. How does the parable encourage us to make faithful use of God's Word? Why is the reward of the second servant comforting to us (vv. 18–19)?

Hosanna to the King!

Read Luke 19:28–40.

Before Jesus humbled Himself and died on the cross (Philippians 2:5–8), He showed that He was the promised King. On Palm Sunday, Jesus rode triumphantly into Jerusalem. Filled with joy, the crowd honored Him as King. The hosannas of the crowd sounded like blasphemy to the Pharisees, who asked that Jesus silence the people.

142. How can we show our loyalty to Jesus as our King? How can we aid Him in entering the hearts of men?

143. What did some of those who shouted hosannas on Palm Sunday say on Good Friday? When does the same thing happen today?

"His Own Received Him Not"

Read Luke 19:41–48.

As the Holy City appeared before Jesus, the Savior burst into tears. Jesus did not weep because He would be crucified but because the people would reject Him as their Savior. Several years before,

Jesus had driven the greedy money changers out of God's house (see John 2:13–16). But His reforms had been in vain. Now, as a sign of judgment, He again cleansed the temple and drove out the merchants.

144. On what other occasion had Jesus wept (John 11:17, 35)? What does this reveal about Jesus?

145. How was the prophecy about Jerusalem fulfilled? Why do we have no excuse if we do not know what peace belongs to us (2 Corinthians 6:2)?

The Enemies' Opposition

Read Luke 20:1–18.

Tuesday of Holy Week was Christ's last day in the temple. It was the last opportunity for the Jews to hear His words. But the leaders of the people ignored His message and His call to repentance. In the parable of the wicked tenants (based on Isaiah 5:1–7), Jesus pictures the love and care God had bestowed upon Israel as His vineyard. But all that God had done for them seemed to have been in vain.

146. Who are the wicked tenants in the vineyard of God today (see Isaiah 5:1–7)?

147. Why is this parable a warning for all Christians (Romans 11:20–22)?

A Plot That Failed

Read Luke 20:19–26.

Although they had failed at earlier attempts to ensnare Jesus, the Pharisees now had a plan they thought would work. Flattering Him, they asked whether God's chosen people should pay taxes to the Roman government, a heathen nation. The Lord saw through the finespun plot. The State is not to interfere in matters of the Church, and the Church is not to meddle in the affairs of the civil government.

148. What governments are instituted by God (Romans 13)? Explain the doctrine of the separation of Church and State (Luke 20:25).

149. What should our attitude be when the government demands obedience in matters that conflict with God's Word (Acts 5:29)?

The Sadducees' Silly Arguments

Read Luke 20:27–40.

The Sadducees were concerned only with life on earth and ridiculed all belief in the hereafter. However, Jesus proved from the story of the burning bush (Exodus 3:6) that there is a resurrection of the body and that the dead are alive to God. The three patriarchs had been dead centuries before Moses, but their souls were with God and continued to live in heaven. All believers who die in the faith will rise again and live in the presence of God (Daniel 12:2; Revelation 14:13).

150. What happens to the soul of the believer at death (see 23:43)?

151. How does St. Paul prove the resurrection of the body in 1 Corinthians 15:12–22?

David's Son and David's Lord

Read Luke 20:41–47.

Jesus silenced His enemies so completely that none of them dared to ask Him any further questions. He compelled the wise scribes to reveal their ignorance of the Scriptures by referring them to Psalm 110. There David addresses the Messiah, his own descendant, as his Lord. Many of the scribes believed that the Messiah would be a mere man. However, Jesus proved that He would also be true God.

152. Why was Christ's question (v. 44) very important? What is the only correct answer (see Matthew 16:16; John 6:68–69)?

153. Why did Jesus warn His disciples against the scribes (vv. 45–47)? What lesson do these words contain for us?

In Closing

Encourage the participants to begin the following activities:

- Work with your congregation's evangelism team to minister to the "Zacchaeuses" in your community;
- Take an active role in your local, state, and national government by voting regularly and by praying for and communicating with your elected leaders;
- Read Luke 21:1–22:71 to prepare for the next lesson.

Close with prayer.

Lesson 11

Our Passover Lamb

Jesus Observes Church Contributions

Read Luke 21:1–4.

Jesus watched people making their contributions. The wealthy gave liberally for the upkeep and support of the temple. However, it was the small contribution of a poor widow that caught His eye. Jesus knew that this poor woman had brought a *real* sacrifice, because she trusted that God would continue to care for her.

154. When is God pleased with our contributions to the Church (1 Corinthians 16:2; 2 Corinthians 9:6–7)?

155. Why should even the poor be encouraged to give to the Church?

Times of Great Tribulation

Read Luke 21:5–19.

Jesus' ministry to the Jews was now ended. He again prophesied the utter destruction of the city and the temple. The disciples thought that Jesus was referring to the end of the world, and they asked when that event would take place. The Lord wants His followers to always be prepared. Jesus has promised that He will take care of His faithful followers until He returns on the Last Day.

156. What should be our attitude toward people who claim to know the date of Christ's return? Why will their predictions always fail?

157. How have Christ's prophecies in verses 9–11 been fulfilled in recent years? Will there ever be perpetual world peace? Explain.

Reading the Signs

Read Luke 21:20–27.

It was especially important that the early Christians escape the destruction of Jerusalem. Christ's prophecy was literally fulfilled in AD 70 when the Romans destroyed the city. All the strange phenomena in the skies and on earth remind us that the world will come to an end. Like the first Christians, we should be constantly ready to meet our Savior (v. 28).

158. What lessons does the destruction of Jerusalem teach us?

159. How is the end of the world described in 2 Peter 3:10–12? In Joel 2:30–31?

Watch and Pray!

Read Luke 21:28–38.

We should not dread the Last Day. All our sorrow and troubles will cease (see Revelation 21:4; Isaiah 35:10; Romans 8:21). Just as the budding trees announce the approach of spring, so all the signs that remind us of Jesus' return should cheer our hearts. But while we await that glorious day, we must carefully avoid the sins of the flesh and the cares of this life. Otherwise, we may lose our faith and be found unprepared when Jesus returns.

160. Why should believers not fear Judgment Day?

161. What is the best way for us to study nature and world events?

The Last Supper

Read Luke 22:1–20.

The time had come for Jesus to celebrate the final Passover with His disciples. This annual festival (see Exodus 12) reminded the Israelites of the sacrifice that Christ would bring for the salvation of the world (John 1:29; 1 Corinthians 5:7). Jesus was now to fulfill what the Passover typified. Jesus gave to His Church the Sacrament of the Lord's Supper. We celebrate this Sacrament often in remembrance of His suffering and death and for the strengthening of our faith (see 1 Corinthians 11:23–29).

162. What great event did the annual Passover commemorate (Exodus 12)? Of what was the Passover lamb a type (1 Corinthians 5:7)?

163. How do the Words of Institution prove that Jesus gives us His true body and blood in the Lord's Supper? Why should we partake of the Sacrament often?

Christ's Last Warnings and Admonitions

Read Luke 22:21–38.

Jesus knew that one of His disciples had become a traitor. At the Passover, the compassionate Savior warned Judas not to commit this foul deed. It was indeed the Father's will that Christ should suffer and die for mankind, but that will not excuse Judas. The other disciples were also in great danger of losing their faith by arguing about places of honor in an earthly kingdom. Peter believed that his faith was strong enough to suffer and die for his Lord, but Jesus knew that Peter would fall in the hour of temptation.

164. Why should we be on our guard against Satan (v. 31)? How can we help our fellow Christians when they fall into sin (v. 32)?

165. Why should we not despair when we know that we have sinned? What comforting assurance does the Bible give us (see 1 John 2:1–2; Hebrews 7:25)?

Gethsemane

Read Luke 22:39–53.

Luke tells us about the dreadful events in the garden. Here we see Jesus on His knees praying that the Father might remove the cup of suffering from Him. But the Savior was perfectly willing to obey His Father and to suffer the punishment for our sins. Our minds cannot grasp the severity of Christ's agony of soul. But our Savior rose victoriously from this battle with Satan. Calmly He went forth to meet His captors, and willingly He permitted His enemies to bind Him and lead Him away to His trial and death.

166. What does Christ's prayer in the garden teach us about the way we should pray? about the value of prayer?

167. How did Jesus demonstrate His love for His enemies?

Insulted by Friend and Foe

Read Luke 22:54–71.

Luke omits the night trial before the Jewish council, but he shows how Peter wounded the heart of Jesus by his denial. Reminded of his sin and of the gracious promise of Jesus, Peter went out and wept bitter tears of repentance. Luke briefly describes the early morning session, when Jesus repeated that He is the Son of God. Though it cost Him His life, Jesus confessed the truth before His enemies.

168. Why is Peter's denial related by all the evangelists with great detail? When might a Christian be tempted to deny the Savior?

169. Why is Peter's repentance comforting to us? Where do we see the loving face of Jesus and receive His assurance of pardon?

In Closing

Encourage the participants to begin the following:

- In contrast to contemporary religious views of Christ's return, discuss the joyful hope believers have on the Last Day;
- Give thanks for the tremendous blessings of forgiveness, life, and salvation that Christ imparts to us in His body and blood in His Supper;
- Read Luke 23:1–24:53 to prepare for the next lesson.

Close with prayer.

Lesson 12

Our Triumphant Savior

"Suffered under Pontius Pilate"

Read Luke 23:1–25.

Early Good Friday morning, the Jewish leaders demanded that the Roman governor put Jesus to death for saying that He was the Son of God. Because this did not impress the Romans, the Jewish leaders falsely accused Jesus of causing a political disturbance and trying to overthrow Roman rule. Pilate knew Jesus was innocent and that the Jews enviously handed Him over (Matthew 27:18). Pilate should have released Jesus immediately, but the governor feared the people he harshly ruled. He foolishly tried to shift the responsibility by sending Jesus to Herod, but Herod returned Him. Pilate then allowed the Jews to choose between Barabbas and Jesus. The crowd demanded that the murderer be set free and that the Lord be crucified.

170. How were the charges against Jesus false (vv. 2, 5; see also Matthew 22:21; 27:18; John 6:15; 18:36)?

171. How does the example of Pilate prove that it is wrong to shirk one's responsibility? to compromise? to put personal interests before duty?

“Crucified”

Read Luke 23:26–43.

The innocent Jesus was led away like a criminal to the place of execution outside the city. Weakened by much suffering, He broke down under the heavy burden of His cross. Simon of Cyrene was compelled to carry it for Him (Mark 15:21). On the way, some women of Jerusalem mourned for Jesus, but the Lord desires to see tears of true repentance (see 22:62). Jesus bore the sins of the world, and in Him we see how God punishes sin. On Calvary, Jesus was crucified between two criminals (Isaiah 53:12). Because He loved sinners and wanted to save them, He willingly permitted Himself to be crucified. The evangelists do not describe the horrible act of crucifixion; they only note the fact.

172. Why was it a great honor and blessing for Simon to bear the cross of Jesus? What should be our attitude to cross bearing? Why?

173. Why are tears of repentance more pleasing to Jesus than pity for Him? What does His suffering teach us about sin? Explain verse 31.

“Dead and Buried”

Read Luke 23:44–56.

From noon until 3 p.m. on Good Friday a darkness covered the whole earth. This darkness symbolized God’s judgment on the world’s Sin-bearer (Isaiah 53:4–12). God forsook His own Son during these dark hours (see Matthew 27:46; Psalm 22:1). Christ was then suffering the punishment for all our sins and paying the awful price for our redemption. When the world was again flooded with light, Jesus knew that His work of saving mankind was finished and accepted by God (John 19:30). With His last word from the cross, He committed His soul to His Father and died a true but voluntary death (Hebrews 2:14–15). Joseph of Arimathea came forward and gave Jesus an honorable burial. The body of the Savior was wrapped in clean linen and laid in a new and costly tomb, there to rest peacefully until its resurrection on Easter morning.

174. What miraculous events took place on Calvary? What lessons do these events teach us?

175. What significance does the death and burial of Jesus have for us?

"The Third Day He Rose Again from the Dead"

Read Luke 24:1–12.

Very early on Easter morning, a group of female disciples went to the grave to complete the embalming of Christ's body. But such an act of love was no longer needed. The sepulcher, which had been carefully sealed and guarded (Matthew 27:66), was now open and empty. Angels in dazzling apparel told the perplexed women that Jesus had returned to life and left the tomb, as He had foretold. The women were to announce this to the other disciples. Hearing the news, Peter and John ran to the sepulcher to investigate the matter. They, too, found the grave empty. Scripture provides sufficient evidence that Jesus rose again and lives. The Church is built upon this truth. This fact assures us that Christ has redeemed us. It fills our hearts with Easter joy!

176. What value would our faith have if Jesus had remained in the grave (see 1 Corinthians 15:14–20)? Why is it important that we believe the Easter Gospel?

177. Mention several proofs of Christ's resurrection. Explain their value. Of what significance is Christ's resurrection for us?

On the Road to Emmaus

Read Luke 24:13–35.

The first Easter Sunday did not find the disciples of Jesus singing hymns of joy, as we do. They were perplexed and sorrowful. In the afternoon, two of them were walking along the road to Emmaus, a village about six miles from Jerusalem. A "stranger" suddenly stepped up to them and asked what they were talking about so seriously. He then quoted and explained the passages of the Old Testament that clearly foretold the Messiah's death and resurrection. By referring the disciples to the Scriptures, Jesus showed that only God's Word can bring a person to faith. When they sat down to eat, their guest acted as host. As He passed the bread to them, the "stranger" revealed Himself, and then He vanished from their sight. Meanwhile, the others had also received new and convincing evidence that Jesus had risen.

178. What are the only means by which God brings a person to faith?

179. How did Jesus show that the Old Testament has great value for us?

The Last Visible Appearances of Jesus

Read Luke 24:36–49.

Late Easter evening, the disciples were still assembled in a room in Jerusalem, hidden behind locked doors for fear of the Jews. Suddenly, Jesus appeared in their midst. He greeted them by saying, "Peace to you." This calmed the disciples and removed their fears that they were seeing a spirit. To convince them that He was alive, He invited them to examine His body, where they could see the marks of His crucifixion. As further evidence, Jesus ate a piece of fish before them. Then He led them into the Scriptures and showed them how He had fulfilled what the prophets had foretold of Him. All the events of His life, which they had witnessed, were necessary for the redemption of the world. Jesus promised to endow them with the power and gifts of the Holy Spirit, who would equip and strengthen them for the great work of the Gospel ministry.

180. What appearances of Jesus are mentioned in John 20 and 21? in 1 Corinthians 15:5–8?

181. How do we know that Christ's resurrected body is the same body that died on the cross? In what respect is it different? What does this teach us about the nature of our bodies after our resurrection (Philippians 3:21)?

"Ascended into Heaven"

Read Luke 24:50–53.

Forty days after Easter, Jesus met with His disciples for the last time on Mount Olivet. Having spoken His farewell words, He raised His hands in blessing over them. In the act of blessing His disciples, the glorified Savior ascended into heaven. The disciples' hearts were filled with joy and thanksgiving. During the next ten days, until Pentecost, they were continually in the temple, praising and blessing God. Joy and praise are heard in the first chapter of Luke's Gospel and in every chapter. Joy and praise and blessing are the closing words of this beautiful Gospel.

182. How was Christ's ascension foretold in the Old Testament (Psalm 47:5–8; 68:18)? How was His ascension typified in 2 Kings 2:11?

183. Why do we call Ascension Day the coronation day of Jesus? Why is it a day of rejoicing among Christians? How can we observe this festival?

In Closing

Encourage participants to begin the following activities:

- Ponder Christ's crucifixion and resurrection with the hymns "Jesus, I Will Ponder Now" (*Lutheran Worship* 109) and "He's Risen, He's Risen" (*Lutheran Worship* 138);
- Enabled by the Holy Spirit, resolve to share the Good News with "all nations": your family members, friends, neighbors, and others who do not yet know Jesus Christ.

Close with prayer.

Leader Notes

This guide is provided as a "safety net," a place to turn for help in answering questions and for enriching discussion. It will not answer every question raised in your class. Please read it, along with the questions, before class. Consult it in class only after exploring the Bible references and discussing what they teach. Please note the different abilities of your class members. Some will easily find the Bible passages listed in this study; others will struggle. To make participation easier, team up members of the class. For example, if a question asks you to look up several passages, assign one passage to one group, the second to another, and so on. Divide the work! Let participants present the answers they discover.

Preparing to Teach Luke

To prepare to lead this study, read through the Book of Luke. You might review the introduction to Luke in the *Concordia Self-Study Bible* or a Bible handbook. A map of Palestine at the time of Jesus would also help.

If you have the opportunity, you will find it helpful to make use of other biblical reference works in the course of your study. These commentaries can be very helpful: Arthur A. Just, Jr., *Luke*, 2 volumes, Concordia Commentary series (St. Louis: Concordia Publishing House, 1996); Victor H. Prange, *Luke*, People's Bible Commentary Series (St. Louis: Concordia Publishing House, 1992); Norval Geldenhuys, *The Gospel of Luke*, The New International Commentary on the New Testament (Grand Rapids: Eerdmans, 1988). Although it is not strictly a commentary, the section on Luke in *The Word Becoming Flesh* by Horace Hummel (St. Louis: Concordia Publishing House, 1979) also contains valuable material for the proper interpretation of this biblical book.

Group Bible Study

Group Bible study means mutual learning from one another under the guidance of a leader. The Bible is an inexhaustible resource. No one person can discover all it has to offer. In any class many eyes see many things, things that can be applied to many life situations. The leader should resist the temptation to "give the answers" and so act as an "authority." This teaching approach stifles participation by individual members and can actually hamper learning. As a general rule don't "give interpretation"; instead, "develop interpreters." In other words, don't explain what the learners can discover by themselves. This is not to say that the leader shouldn't share insights and information gained by his or her class members during the lesson, engage them in meaningful sharing and discussion, or lead them to a summary of the lesson at the close.

Have a chalkboard and chalk or newsprint and marker available to emphasize significant points of the lesson. Rephrase your inquiries or the inquiries of participants as questions, problems, or issues. This provokes thought. Keep discussion to the point. List on the chalkboard or newsprint the answers given. Then determine the most vital points made in the discussion. Ask additional questions to fill gaps.

The aim of every Bible study is to help people grow spiritually, not merely in biblical and theological knowledge, but in Christian thinking and living. This means growth in Christian attitudes, insights, and skills for Christian living. The focus of this course must be the Church and the world of our day. The guiding question will be this: What does the Lord teach us for life today through Luke?

Teaching the New Testament

Teaching a New Testament Letter that was originally written for and read to first-century Christians can become merely ancient history if not applied to life in our times. Leaders need to understand the time and culture in which the Letter was written. They need to understand the historical situation of the Early Church and the social and cultural setting in which that Church existed. Such background information can clarify the original purpose and meaning of the Letter and shed light on its meaning for Christians today. For this reason, Bible commentaries and other reference works are indispensable when it comes to leading Bible studies.

Teaching the Bible can easily degenerate into mere moralizing, in which "do-goodism" or rules become substitutes for the Gospel, and sanctification is confused with justification. Actually, justified sinners are moved not by Law, but by God's grace to a totally new life. Their faith is always at work for Christ in every context of life. Meaningful, personal Christianity consists of a loving trust in God that is evidenced in love for others. Having experienced God's free grace and forgiveness, Christians daily work in their world to reflect the will of God for people in every area of human endeavor.

Christian leaders are Gospel-oriented, not Law-oriented; they distinguish between the two. Both Law and Gospel are necessary. The Gospel will mean nothing unless we first have been crushed by the Law and see our sinfulness. There is no genuine Christianity if faith is not followed by lives pleasing to God. In fact, genuine faith is inseparable from life. The Gospel alone gives us the new heart that causes us to love God and our neighbor.

Pace Your Teaching

The lessons in this course of study are designed for a study session of at least an hour in length. If it is the desire and intent of the class to complete an entire lesson each session, it will be necessary for you to summarize the content of certain answers or biblical references in order to preserve time. Asking various class members to look up different Bible passages and to read them aloud to the rest of the class will save time over having every class member look up each reference.

Also, you may not want to cover every question in each lesson. This may lead to undue haste and frustration. Be selective. Pace your teaching. Spend no more than 5–10 minutes opening the lesson. During the lesson, get the sweep of meaning. Occasionally stop to help the class gain understanding of a word or concept. Allow approximately 5 minutes for "Closing" and announcements.

Should your group have more than a one-hour class period, you can take it more leisurely. But do not allow any lesson to drag and become tiresome. Keep it moving. Keep it alive. Keep it meaningful. Eliminate some questions and restrict yourself to those questions most meaningful to the members of the class. If most members study the text at home, they can report their findings, and the time gained can be applied to relating the lesson to life.

Good Preparation

Good preparation by the leader usually affects the pleasure and satisfaction the class will experience.

Suggestions to the Leader for Using the Study Guide

The Lesson Pattern

This set of lessons is designed to aid *Bible study*, that is, to aid a consideration of the written Word of God, with discussion and personal application growing out of the text at hand.

The typical lesson is divided into these sections:

1. Theme Verse
2. Objectives
3. Questions and Answers
4. Closing

The theme verse and objectives give you, the leader, assistance in arousing the interest of the group in the concepts of the lesson. Focus on stimulating minds. Do not linger too long over the introductory remarks.

The questions and answers provide the real spadework necessary for Bible study. Here the class digs, uncovers, and discovers; it gets the facts and observes them. Comments from the leader are needed only to the extent that they help the group understand the text. The questions in this guide, corresponding to sections within the text, are intended to help the participants discover the meaning of the text.

Having determined what the text says, the class is ready to apply the message. Having heard, read, marked, and learned the Word of God, they can proceed to digest it inwardly through discussion, evaluation, and application. This is done, as this guide suggests, by taking the truths found in Scripture and applying them to the world, and Christianity in general, and then to one's personal Christian life. Class time may not permit discussion of all questions and topics. In preparation you may need to select one or two and focus on them. Close the session by reviewing one important truth from the lesson.

Remember, the Word of God is sacred, but this study guide is not. The notes in this section offer only guidelines and suggestions. Do not hesitate to alter the guidelines or substitute others to meet your needs and the needs of the participants. Adapt your teaching plan to your class and your class period.

Good teaching directs the learner to discover for himself or herself. For the teacher this means directing the learner, not giving the learner answers. Directing understanding takes preparation. Choose the verses that should be looked up in Scripture ahead of time. What discussion questions will you ask? At what points? Write them in the margin of your study guide. Involve class members, but give them clear directions. What practical actions might you propose for the week following the lesson? Which of the items do you consider most important for your class?

Consider how you can best use your teaching period. Do you have 45 minutes, an hour, or an hour and a half? If time is short, what should you cut? Learn to become a wise steward of class time.

Plan a brief opening devotion, using members of the class. And be sure to take time to summarize the lesson, or have a class member do it.

Remember to pray frequently for yourself and your class. May God the Holy Spirit bless your study and your leading of others into the comforting truths of God's Christ-centered Word.

Lesson 1

The Most Wonderful Child

Theme verse: *Therefore the child to be born will be called holy—the Son of God.*

Luke 1:35

Objectives

By the power of the Holy Spirit working through God's Word, we will

- Learn from Zechariah and Elizabeth, who proved their faith by living God-pleasing lives;
- Reflect on the hope-filled yearning of Old Testament believers as they awaited the coming Messiah and rejoiced at His birth;
- Give thanks for the good news of great joy announced by the angel and of which we partake in Word and Sacrament.

1. The leader may begin this course by discussing the introduction to Luke's Gospel. Ask participants to read the preface (vv. 1–4). Stress that Luke was written especially for the Gentiles. Luke shows God's preparations for the coming Savior. In reality, the whole Old Testament was a period of preparation (advent) for the birth of the Messiah.

2. Childless Old Testament believers like Sarah, Rachel, and Hannah, although they later conceived and gave birth, prayerfully resigned themselves to God's gracious will (Psalm 34:19; Hebrews 12:11). New Testament believers do the same.

3. We pray, "Thy will be done." Jesus promises that He both hears and answers the prayers we make in His name—that is, through faith in Him. Sometimes, as in the case of Zechariah and Elizabeth, His answer is "Yes," even after a prolonged wait. Sometimes His answer is "No." Regardless, His will is best for us.

4. It is a sin not to take God at His Word. People sometimes say, "I can't believe this statement of the Bible because I can't understand it. I will not accept it because it does not seem to agree with science

and experience." Jesus refused to give unbelievers the sign they asked for (Luke 11:16–29). But God mercifully helps His children.

5. When uncertain about a truth expressed in Scripture, continue studying the Bible, praying for the Holy Spirit's help and guidance. Consult with your pastor. Believe the Word, even though you cannot understand and explain it (1 Corinthians 13:12).

6. The Bible clearly speaks about Mary's virginity at the time of Christ's conception and how important this fact is for us (see also Hebrews 4:15; John 8:46). Because of His supernatural conception, Jesus did not inherit (original) sin (Romans 5:12, 19). The denial of the virginity of Mary at Christ's conception is a tacit denial of His divinity.

7. Refer to verses 28 and 30 ("favor" means "grace") and verse 47 (needed a Savior; see also Matthew 4:10). Through the Word, God gave Mary the gift of faith in the work to which God called her. Christians are also given faith through the Word (Gospel and the Sacraments) so that they may serve the Lord in their vocations. Like Mary, they acknowledge their sinfulness and God's grace.

8. Note the emphasis on salvation, deliverance, the remission of sins, and a godly life. A "horn" signifies strength or power (see Psalm 18:2; 1 Kings 22:11). "Dayspring" means "sunrising" (Isaiah 60), or "morning star" (Revelation 22:16; Malachi 4:2).

9. Natural man is spiritually blind and dead (see Isaiah 60; Acts 26:18). The Gospel illuminates the hearts that "sit in darkness" (Luke 1:79) and fills them with spiritual light (1 Peter 2:9; 2 Corinthians 4:6). Note how Zechariah's hymn expresses Christian faith, joy, hope, and peace that come only through the arrival of God's grace-filled presence (Isaiah 60:1–3).

10. Bethlehem was the birthplace of David (1 Samuel 16:1–13). Both Joseph (as foster father) and Mary (as Jesus' mother) were descendents of King David. Thus, legally, through Joseph (Matthew 1:16–17; Luke 2:4), and biologically, through Mary (Luke 1:32–33), Jesus is David's Son (Matthew 1:1; 22:41–42). Jesus' birth in Bethlehem fulfills Micah's prophecy (5:2) and further proves the Bible's reliability.

11. The Son of God left the riches of heaven and took on the poverty of humanity by becoming man (2 Corinthians 8:9; John 1:14). He did this so that freed from sin by His life, death, and resurrection, we might enjoy the riches of heaven. The servant attitude of the Master is also that of the believer (Philippians 2:5–11). The angel's message is

"good news of a great joy" (Luke 2:10) because through this child God richly grants "peace" (2:14).

12. Christ is not found today in the Bethlehem manger; He is found in His Gospel and Sacraments (Matthew 28:19–20; Mark 16:15–16; Luke 22:19–20; John 20:30–31). People do not "find" Jesus because, instead of hearing the Gospel, they trust in their obedience to the Law or human reasoning (Romans 10:5–21).

13. The Christian takes every opportunity to tell others about Jesus because "faith comes from hearing, and hearing through the word of Christ" (Romans 10:17).

14. As our substitute, Jesus fully and perfectly submitted to God's Law to keep and fulfill it for us (Galatians 4:4–5). Jesus' circumcision and presentation in the temple bear witness to this fact (Luke 2:21–24; see also Exodus 13:2, 12). The circumcision also served as the occasion for naming the child; Jesus' name (and its meaning: "Yahweh saves") given by the angel Gabriel (Luke 1:31) points to His divine origin. The temple visit also served as the end of Mary's purification, or forty days following childbirth, at which time she would offer an appropriate sacrifice (see Leviticus 12:6–8).

15. The Nunc Dimittis (or "Now, let depart") serves as a post-communion canticle (*LW*, pp. 152–3, 173–4, 193; *TLH*, p. 29; *HS98*, p. 14). Simeon's song is a wonderful hymn of joyful trust in God's Word of promise. Just as Simeon and Anna beheld (and in Simeon's case, touched) the Lord in the temple, so, too, do we depart with thanks following our experience with the risen Christ in His Word and in His true body and true blood of His holy Supper.

16. When Jewish boys were three, their parents began religious instruction with simple prayers and Scripture passages (Deuteronomy 6:6–7). At six, they would attend a synagogue school (2 Timothy 3:15). At twelve, they became a "son of the Law" and were obliged to attend the festivals. Contemporary confirmation instruction parallels these expectations by recognizing the ability and necessity of adolescent boys and girls growing into and accepting greater spiritual responsibility for themselves. However, confirmation is never the end of the study of God's Word.

17. Jesus' first words in Luke's Gospel are no sign of disrespect to His earthly parents, but rather show that even at this age He recognized His deity. Mary gently chided Jesus for causing them worry; Jesus gently chided His mother for assuming the Son could be "lost" in His Father's house.

Lesson 2

Galilean Ministry

Theme verse: *And a voice came from heaven, "You are My beloved Son; with You I am well pleased."*

Luke 3:22

Objectives

By the power of the Holy Spirit working through God's Word, we will

- Rejoice that Jesus publicly became our substitute and sin-bearer at His Baptism and that we became God's children in our Baptism;
- Learn that Jesus overcame Satan for us and that He showed us how we can resist temptation with the help of God's Word;
- Resolve to take time to read, hear, and apply God's Word in our vocations and the work we render for Jesus.

18. Matthew vividly describes John's unique appearance (Matthew 3:4). Isaiah's language evokes road building (the clearing of rocks and debris and the leveling of land), which figuratively portrays the preparations representatives would make in order to "pave the way" of an arriving king (Isaiah 40:3–5). John is King Jesus' "messenger" (Malachi 3:1), a latter prophet "Elijah" (4:5–6), and the living fulfillment of Isaiah's prophecy (Luke 3:4–6). In anticipation of Jesus' arrival, John called for genuine repentance, which is more than sorrow for sin or regret. It is a change of heart and life and includes faith.

19. To our detriment, we deflect the Law in a sermon by taking offense or by thinking, "That's not meant for me; it's meant for so-and-so." However, we are called upon to apply both Law *and* Gospel to ourselves and to our daily lives. The preparatory seasons of Advent and Lent serve as seasons of repentance preceding the seasons of joy (Christmas and Easter).

20. Jesus (the Son; Luke 1:35), the Spirit descending in the form of a dove, and the Father's voice from heaven (both 3:22) show the Holy Trinity most vividly. So, too, does Gabriel's birth announcement to Mary (Luke 1:35; "Holy Spirit," "Most High," "Son of God"; see also Acts 1:7–9, written by Luke, where Jesus refers to both the "Father" and the "Holy Spirit"). Our Baptism brings us into a saving relationship with the Holy Trinity (1 Peter 3:21). Through water and the Word (the name of the Holy Trinity; Matthew 28:19) we receive the forgiveness of sins and the Holy Spirit (Acts 2:38–39; 22:16) and are reborn into God's family (John 3:5–6; Titus 3:5–7).

21. Christ's Baptism was not only His public identification with sinners (2 Corinthians 5:21), but also His indication of complete consecration and submission to God's will.

Through our Baptism, we are united with Christ in both His death and resurrection for the forgiveness of our sins (Romans 6:4) and receive the "clothing" of Christ's righteousness (Galatians 3:26–27).

22. Notice that Satan approached Jesus in the same manner as he did Eve: through the needs of the body. Satan casts doubt on the validity of God's Word or our understanding of it ("Did God actually say?" [Genesis 3:1]). The same happens today when macroevolution is accepted as a substitute (or a corollary) of the biblical account of creation. In contrast to Eve (and Adam), however, Jesus resisted Satan's temptation by faithfully applying God's Word. This is why Satan failed.

23. Satan perverts and twist God's good creation so that what is given by Him as gift is used to tempt us to the peril of our souls (1 John 2:15–17; 1 Timothy 6:9; Genesis 3:1; see also 1 Peter 5:8). Knowing the Bible through regular worship attendance, Bible study, and Bible memorization will help us overcome temptations (Psalm 119:105; Colossians 3:16; James 4:7–8; 1 Peter 5:8–9).

24. According to Isaiah's prophecy, the work of the Spirit-anointed Messiah would include preaching and miracles, the latter serving as signs bearing witness of and drawing attention to the message that was proclaimed (the "good news" [4:18] declaring "the year of the Lord's favor" [4:19]; see also 2:10–11).

25. The widow of Zarephath showed that she was a believer, and that she accepted Elijah's ministry, by obeying God's Word through the mouth of the prophet (1 Kings 17:9–24). Likewise Naaman who, after some prodding by his servants, dipped himself in the Jordan and was cleansed of leprosy showed his belief (2 Kings 5:1–19). Both were

Gentiles. Jesus referred the Nazarenes to these Old Testament accounts to imply that if the Jews refused to believe on Him, many Gentiles would nevertheless accept the Gospel (Matthew 8:11–12).

26. The word *synagogue* or *synagogues*, where Jesus frequently preached, appears in 4:15, 16, 20, 28, 33, 38, and 44. Jesus' miracles lead people to hear His preaching, which is why He was sent (Luke 4:43). Those who received miraculous healings (or were raised from the dead) at the hand of Jesus were indeed cured (or made alive); they would nevertheless become ill again and die. However, those who believe in Him through His message receive eternal life (John 20:31), and have the promise of perfect, resurrected bodies that will never become ill or die (1 Corinthians 15:42–57).

27. Luke has many references to healings of demoniacs, those possessed by demons. Two appear in this chapter (see also 8:26–39). Evil spirits became especially evident through Christ's dealings with men. While there will always be some people who deny that Jesus is true God, the devil and demons acknowledge His authority (see James 2:19). Satan controls unbelievers through their unbelief. His power can be broken only by the Word of God, through faith (1 Peter 5:8). Faith in Jesus Christ protects us from the "flaming darts of the evil one" (Ephesians 6:16).

28. Many believers aided Jesus in His proclamation of the kingdom of God: the Magi, whose gifts aided the holy family's sojourn into Egypt (Matthew 2); the woman who anointed Jesus' feet with her tears (Luke 7:36–38); the woman who anointed Jesus' head with oil (Mark 14:1–9); the owners who lent Jesus their donkey to enter Jerusalem (Luke 19:28–35); the man who lent the disciples a room for the Last Supper (Mark 14:13–15); and Joseph of Arimathea, who allowed Jesus to borrow his tomb temporarily (Matthew 27:57–61).

29. When done in faith in our Lord Jesus, all that we do is God pleasing, including our daily labors. In our vocations, and as we assist Jesus in the proclamation of His Gospel through the use of our time, talents, and treasures, we can be assured that our work "is not in vain" (1 Corinthians 15:58). We cannot allow low attendance or seemingly poor results to cause us to grieve; nor can we allow appearances of "success" at churches other than our own to discourage us. Why compare? When we are faithful to God and His Word in our proclamation and in our deeds, we know that He will offer His blessings.

Lesson 3

Jesus, the Messiah

Theme verse: *"But that you may know that the Son of Man has authority on earth to forgive sins"—He said to the man who was paralyzed—"I say to you, rise, pick up your bed and go home."*

Luke 5:24

Objectives

By the power of the Holy Spirit working through God's Word, we will

- Give thanks that no matter how great our needs, Jesus can help—He is pleased to do so in answer to our prayers;
- Affirm that our greatest need is forgiveness of sins, and that He who heals the soul will save also the body;
- Ponder that the members of Christ's kingdom rejoice in their salvation and that good works are the necessary fruits of faith.

30. Naaman, commander of the king of Syria's army, was cleansed of leprosy by washing in the waters of the Jordan seven times (2 Kings 5). Later, on the way to Jerusalem, Jesus healed ten lepers, of whom only one returned to offer thanks (Luke 17:11–19).

We refer to sin as a spiritual leprosy because (a) it has entirely corrupted our nature and (b) it is incurable except by the divine touch of the Savior (means of grace). We have the assurance of a true spiritual cleansing through God's Word and Sacraments.

31. Jesus referred the thankful man to the priests (a) in order to obtain the legal certificate of his cleansing, the priests functioning as public health officials, and, (b) more importantly, to provide the priests a living testimony that He was the promised Messiah.

32. The first and greatest need of every person is the forgiveness of sins. There is no peace without it, even with otherwise perfect health. The Pharisees and scribes felt no sinfulness and hated the word *forgiveness*. In sullen silence, they grumbled in their hearts and

accused Jesus of blasphemy. They refused to accept the truth that Jesus is God. To forgive sin and to heal a sick person with a word are equally impossible to a mere man. Only God can do both.

Jesus graciously assures us that our sins are forgiven through His means of grace: His Gospel proclaimed and read, Absolution, and the Sacraments of Baptism and Holy Communion.

33. By this and other miracles, Jesus offered visible proof that He is God (vv. 24–26). He calls Himself by the messianic title "Son of Man" (used eighty-four times in the New Testament; see Daniel 7:13–14). The healing also proved the power to forgive. The man was healed spiritually and physically. He and the people who were not prejudiced against Jesus glorified God for what they had experienced. Our response as we experience God's grace in Jesus Christ is also thanks and praise to God, and loving service to our neighbor.

34. Levi's first public act as a disciple was to prepare a feast honoring Christ. He received or adopted the name Matthew. Later, Matthew wrote one of our four Gospels.

35. All believers, in spite of outward circumstances, are justified by faith and have peace with God through their Savior (Romans 5:1). Because Christ through His sufferings and death has reconciled us to the Father, we have cause to rejoice always (Philippians 4:4).

36. Jesus reminded His hearers that David did not sin in eating the showbread because his was an emergency (1 Samuel 21:6). True, the showbread could be eaten only by priests (Leviticus 22:10) and, by appearances, their national hero and saint had violated the letter of the Law (Leviticus 24:5–9). But David had not violated its spirit in this case of necessity. He and his companions received the showbread that had already served its function in the temple with approval from the priests. Jesus clearly teaches here that the ceremonial law was not to be interpreted in a legalistic manner, and that it is always lawful to do good to others and to preserve life (Luke 6:9).

Luke omits the second argument of Jesus (Matthew 12:5). Jesus is the Lord of the Sabbath (Colossians 2:16–17). He is the giver of the Law and therefore can both interpret and abolish it.

37. Jesus healed the man whose hand had atrophied ("withered," "shriveled"). Perhaps this was due to a disease, an accident, or was the result of a congenital defect. Regardless, the Pharisees were clearly more interested in the rigorous outward observance of the Law than in the best interests of the man. Jesus used this occasion to demonstrate His power as the divine Son of God, His love and care for those who

suffer, and the insufferable pride and haughtiness of the unbelieving Pharisees.

The Law not only forbids the doing of certain wicked things, it also commands doing good deeds (Luke 10:28, 37; 6:31; see also the Ten Commandments). Jesus frequently healed on the Sabbath (see 13:13–14; 14:3–4; John 9:14–16). This is the lesson Jesus teaches through this healing miracle: While many people pride themselves on never having done any great wrong, they are nevertheless condemned by always refusing to do anything right.

38. The disciples chosen as apostles were **Simon Peter** and **Andrew** (John 1:36–42); **James** and **John**, sons of Zebedee and Salome (Luke 9:54; Acts 12:2); **Philip** (John 1:43–45; 12:20–22, not the evangelist mentioned in Acts 6:5; 8:5, 26–40); **Bartholomew**, identified with Nathanael of Cana (John 1:47); **Matthew**, the former tax collector Levi and author of the first Gospel (Luke 5:27; Matthew 9:9); **Thomas**, called Didymus, "Twin" (John 11:16; 20:28); **James**, son of Alphaeus, known later as James the Less or the "Just"; **Simon**, the Canaanite, called Zelotes, the "Zealot"; **Judas** (called "the brother of James," but according to the original text more probably the son of an unknown James) also bore the names Thaddaeus or Lebbaeus (Matthew 10:3); and **Judas Iscariot**, the man of Kerioth in Judea, the traitor (John 13:2, 18).

It is this latter Judas, who betrayed our Lord, who does not appear in Acts 1:13. Matthias was chosen to replace him (1:26). The apostle Paul was later added to the apostolic band (9:1–15). His ministry, given to him by Christ Himself (v. 15), was accepted by the other apostles (Galatians 2:1–10).

39. Today, pastors are called into their offices through the Christian congregation.

40. Matthew has eight Beatitudes, Luke has only four. Luke omits the "meek," "merciful," "pure in heart," and "peacemakers."

41. Unbelievers can judge only by what they see in this life (human standards). They cannot see the blessedness of faith coexisting with a poverty of spirit, hunger for God's grace and forgiveness, sadness over sins, or ridicule for faith in Jesus. They do not understand the theology of the cross, but only the theology of glory. Unaided by the Holy Spirit (1 Corinthians 2:14), they do not experience true joy in this life, nor will they experience it in eternity.

42. Love is more than avoidance of sinful deeds. The love of a believer embraces all people, also his enemies. Only a regenerated

person can love in the sense and spirit that God requires (see Luke 23:34; Acts 7:60). Jesus' emphasis is on "doing good," regardless of the person. In Luke 6:29, Jesus uses a proverbial expression to show that a believer should be willing to suffer insults, injury, and loss of property rather than let bitter feelings rule the heart. Loving our neighbor as ourselves means not only avoiding evil, but also being active in doing good (1 John 3:17).

43. The love and mercy of God through Jesus Christ move the believer to act on behalf of the neighbor (Romans 12:1–2). Unbelievers cannot fulfill the requirements of the Sermon on the Mount because they are not motivated by God's mercy in Christ. Lacking faith, unbelievers cannot please God, even by accomplishing outwardly the works demanded by the Sermon on the Mount (Hebrews 11:6).

44. In order for a building to last, it must have a good foundation. Christians should be like lighthouses (Matthew 5:14). The only solid rock for our spiritual and eternal life is Christ and His Word. He is our cornerstone (1 Peter 2:4–8), upon which we are being built, with the apostles' and prophets' words serving as the foundation (Ephesians 2:19–22). Building on human opinions, the latest scientific or psychological "discoveries," or the teachings of errorists and false teachers who claim the mantle of "Christianity" but are in reality heretics is dangerous. This material will fall to pieces now or on Judgment Day. Nothing spurious in religion will stand the final test.

45. The Jews praised the centurion for his love of their nation and for his building them a synagogue. Jesus praised him for his faith. The centurion built upon the right foundation and produced real fruits of faith, as required in the Sermon of the Mount (i.e., love, humility, compassion, sincerity, trust). While we are saved by God's grace through faith in Christ without our works, we do produce the works that God has prepared for us to do (Ephesians 2:8–10).

Lesson 4

The Compassionate Savior

Theme verse: *And He said, "Young man, I say to you, arise." And the dead man sat up and began to speak, and Jesus gave him to his mother.*

Luke 7:14–15

Objectives

By the power of the Holy Spirit working through God's Word, we will

- Learn that when doubts arise in our hearts we should go to Jesus in His Word;
- Rejoice that penitent sinners always have free access to Jesus and receive assurance of His forgiveness;
- Take comfort in our trials and afflictions, since God uses them to bring us to Jesus, who strengthens and comfort us.

46. In addition to other assistance, when believers comfort the sad and bereaved with words of Scripture, they are doing what Jesus did at Nain. Jesus dries our tears (Revelation 7:17). That is a good reason for knowing many Bible passages by heart.

47. It shows Jesus' power over death (John 11:25–26; see 1 Thessalonians 4:13–17). This is also vividly illustrated in the raising of Lazarus (John 11:43–44).

48. John had spent several months in prison. His disciples who visited him reported what Jesus was doing. Some people think that John became weak in faith while in prison and began to doubt that Jesus was the Messiah because He did not establish a visible kingdom. Others, however, believe that John never wavered in his faith but that he sent his disciples to Jesus for their sake. This seems to agree better with verse 24, that John was not "a reed shaken by the wind." John at least did the right thing. If a person wants to know the truth about Jesus, he or she should not rely on the opinions of others but go directly to Jesus, to His Word, in which He speaks to us.

49. Whenever we are perplexed or harassed by doubts, we should turn to the Bible (John 5:39). The same holds true for those who express doubts about Jesus being the Son of God and Savior of the world. The Gospel was written down as a means of grace to convey eternal life through the message about Jesus. Our experience with Him in Word and Sacrament leads us to tell others about Him, just like the early disciples did (John 1:45).

50. In contrast to the Old Testament prophets, we have the whole Bible, can see redemption completed in Jesus Christ, and can know all that God has revealed to us in His Word. Naturally, these privileges bring corresponding responsibilities (see Luke 12:48). Like the prophets, we should search deeply into the Scriptures to see where Christ reveals Himself in types, prophetic signs foreshadowing His person or work (the bronze serpent: see Numbers 21:8–9 and John 3:14) and prophecies (Abraham's seed: see Genesis 12:7 and Galatians 3:16).

51. When pastors speak to us the Word of God, we are obliged to listen and observe it. Rejecting God's Word from our pastors is a rejection of Christ Himself (Luke 10:16). However, we can take great assurance in knowing that when our pastors speak to us God's Word we are hearing the voice of our Savior. When our pastors declare that God has reconciled us to Himself through the death and resurrection of His Son, we are to believe this as the very voice of heaven (2 Corinthians 5:20; see also Matthew 18:18; John 20:23; Augsburg Confession XXV 3).

52. Christians' proper attitude toward the fallen is one of humble charity and forgiveness. This does not mean that Christians overlook sin or that they substitute contemporary morality for God's exacting Law found in His Word. Rather, they love others because they themselves were first loved by God in Christ Jesus (1 John 4:10). All people need God's Word of forgiveness in Christ, but certain groups especially need it, such as prisoners, the institutionalized, those suffering from terminal diseases, the dying, the homebound, the poor, those who have been abused, and others.

53. This text (v. 47) and other passages (1 John 4:10, 19; Romans 5:8, 10) do not teach that our love moves God to forgive us, but that God has already canceled our debts (v. 42; 2 Corinthians 5:19–21). Our love to God is the evidence of our faith. The woman demonstrated her thankful faith by her works. Her love showed she recognized the

forgiveness given her. God's great love for all sinners is the reason for His great forgiveness through Christ Jesus (John 3:16; 1 John 3:1).

54. Jesus proclaimed "the good news of the kingdom of God" (8:1), which generates faith in the hearts of hearers (Romans 10:17). It is important that we hear God's Word with humble hearts (Ecclesiastes 5:1–2). Satan is always on the alert to spoil our hearing. He tries to make us inattentive, fills our hearts with distracting thoughts, and helps us to forget what we have heard. (see 1 Peter 5:8–9). Luke records several of the many women who assisted Jesus' ministry by providing "out of their means" (Luke 8:2–3).

55. Jesus' explains His parable (8:4–8) immediately after delivering it (vv. 9–15). While God's Word is "living and active" (Hebrews 4:12) and accomplishes everything the Lord desires (Isaiah 55:11), not all people are benefited by hearing and reading it.

Some people hear the Word with hearts that have not been prepared to receive it. Because they do not repent of their sins and desire a Savior, the preaching of the Gospel is wasted on them, like seed that falls on hard, uncultivated ground. Others are conscious of sin and rejoice when they hear that they have a Savior, but their hearts are like a field that has only a thin covering of good soil over hard rock. They make a good beginning, but they do not continue in daily repentance. Still others want to be saved by Jesus but allow the cares and pleasures of life to fill and control their hearts. The love of money and pleasure are like thorns that choke the seed of the Gospel.

56. Illumined by the Gospel, Christians are to shine as lights. They illumine others with the glory of God's grace revealed in Jesus Christ (see Isaiah 60:1; Matthew 5:14–16).

57. Jesus calls all those who believe in Him and put His words into practice His "mother and brothers" (i.e., His family). Earthly relationships are for this life only. With Jesus and our fellow believers (whether alive or dead) we are united eternally. This close, familial connection to our Savior and to others trusting in Him is a source of great comfort in times of trial or sorrow. Paul also calls us "fellow citizens with the saints and members of the household of God" (Ephesians 2:19), and Peter says that we "are a chosen race, a royal priesthood, a holy nation, a people for His own possession . . . God's people [who have] received mercy" (1 Peter 2:9–10).

58. When it comes to the care of His children, God does not "fall asleep on the job" (see Psalm 121:3–4). Even while asleep, Jesus continued caring for His disciples. Even had the boat sunk, His

followers would have had nothing to fear—not even death (Romans 14:8). In the midst of our troubles, we can be assured of God's help through His many promises of protection, love, and grace recorded in His Word.

59. Lack of trust is a sin against the First Commandment (Proverbs 3:5). Even strong Christians can grow weak in faith and fall. This serves as both a comfort and a warning (1 Corinthians 10:12–13). A weak faith is still faith (Isaiah 42:3), but it is dangerous to have a weak faith. Jesus often chided His disciples for not having a strong faith. Trials should drive us to prayer and God's Word.

60. This text reveals the great power and the evil purposes of the devil. Satan enjoys torturing God's creatures (vv. 27, 29, 33). He rules in the hearts of all unbelievers. Jesus came to destroy the works of the devil and deliver all people from his bondage (see Isaiah 61:1; Luke 4:18). That is why we need not fear the devil; he is already defeated.

61. Answers may vary. For many, as for the Gerasenes, worldly possessions are far more important than the forgiveness of sins and eternal life that is available only in Jesus Christ. Those who love money—not those who merely possess it—run the danger of losing their faith altogether (1 Timothy 6:9–10). Devoted solely to acquiring and maintaining their wealth, like the rich man in the parable, they do not prepare for the life to come (Luke 12:20–21).

62. Although delayed by healing the woman first, Jesus heard and answered Jairus's prayer. This should teach us about the importance of both patience and persistence in our prayers. Prayer has no power of its own; it is our communication to our gracious God. However, God hears every prayer we utter, even in the silence of our hearts, and answers every prayer, even if that answer is no. Because only God is all-knowing and only He can work toward our good, we pray as our Lord taught us: "Thy will be done."

63. Although believers sometimes fear death, they have no reason to do so. Life for a Christian means serving God by serving others; death means being in the heavenly presence of Christ and the souls of believers who have preceded us (Philippians 1:21–23). Our confidence is in the resurrection of all flesh, when on the Last Day we, in our own glorious bodies, will behold our Redeemer with our own eyes (Job 19:35–27). The Scriptures sometimes refer to death euphemistically as a "sleep" for the body (see John 11:11; 1 Corinthians 15:18), which will be awakened by the returning Savior as if from a slumber.

Lesson 5

Disciples Trained for Service

Theme verse: *Then He said to them, "But who do you say that I am?" And Peter answered, "The Christ of God."*

Luke 9:20

Objectives

By the power of the Holy Spirit working through God's Word, we will

- Affirm that Jesus wants His disciples to work in His kingdom and that He equips them for this work;
- Ponder that as believers suffer for Jesus' sake, they are strengthened by knowing that they have eternal life;
- Resolve that while no one is saved by keeping the Law, nevertheless, we strive to keep the Law because of God's love for us in Christ Jesus.

64. Opinions about miracles (and supposed miracle workers) may vary. Certainly we cannot stand for Christian "healers" who are in reality charlatans and hucksters. However, we can give thanks to God for spontaneous healing (which physicians recognize), as well as the healing that takes place most often—through the work of doctor, nurse, therapist, technician, and pharmacist and through prayer (James 5:14–16). Whether God in His providential care wills genuine physical miracles or not, the Church relies on the powerful Word of God for the ultimate miracle, the forgiveness of sins through faith in Jesus Christ (Romans 10:17).

65. The apostles were to rely on the kindness of their hearers for their sustenance and not on their own labors outside of the ministry (Luke 9:3–5). Likewise, God has commanded the Church to meet the needs of her servants, the pastors (1 Corinthians 9:14; Galatians 6:6). Congregations should see that pastors be accorded compensation (cash, housing allowance, insurance, educational expenses, etc.) that provides a suitable standard of living for them and their families. Miserliness or

stinginess in the matter of pastoral or church-worker compensation is a sign of a weak faith (Luke 16:13; 1 Corinthians 9:7–12; 16:1–2; 1 Timothy 5:17–18; 6:17–19).

66. God daily works miracles to sustain our lives. We should pray for these material gifts, even as Jesus did (Matthew 6:11), and we should be content with the fare that God sets before us. God gives us more than we need so that we can share with others. In Psalm 37, David reminds us of God's constant provision and care. We may not have everything we want, but God supplies us with what we actually need, and He wants us to thank Him for His gifts and not misuse or waste them.

67. Like their Lord (v. 16), Christians give thanks before (and after) meals as a recognition that everything comes from the Father's gracious hand.

68. The disciples witnessed a foretaste of the heavenly glory and an irrefutable confirmation of the deity of Jesus by His transfiguration (see John 1:14; 2 Peter 1:16–18). We, too, shall see Jesus in this state either in heaven or on the Last Day (John 17:24). That the disciples recognized Moses and Elijah suggests that in the immediate presence of the divine glory we will recognize other believers in heaven (1 Corinthians 13:12).

69. Peter wanted to prolong his experience of God's glory by building tabernacles, or booths made of limbs of trees, to shelter Jesus and His guests. However, Jesus had other plans. The Father's arresting "listen to Him!" drew the disciples back to the conversation of Jesus, Moses, and Elijah, which centered upon Jesus' "departure": His exodus, or death, for the salvation of sinners. In Jesus, the person of God's Son tabernacled with us in human flesh, and instead of resting under the limbs of trees crafted as a shelter, He was nailed to a tree, laboring under the sins of the world. The Father's words echo in our ears as we are led from our self-devised "doing" for Jesus to listening to Him speak to us in His Word.

70. The sacrificial death of Jesus (along with His bodily resurrection) is the central proclamation of the Gospel and is the lifeblood of the Church (1 Corinthians 2:2). By His death, Christ accomplished our redemption (1 Peter 1:18–19; 2 Corinthians 5:19–21). We should frequently remind ourselves of Jesus' cruel sufferings and death on the cross because (a) it will aid us in seeing the enormity of our sins, costing the very life of the Son of God; (b) it is the message of our salvation and forgiveness through Jesus' broken body and

poured-out blood; and (c) it will instill within us a sense of the Master's humility and self-sacrifice as we seek to convey His message of life and salvation to a lost world that God loves (John 3:16).

71. The disciples were not to stop other believers in their desire to alleviate suffering by the use of Jesus' name. In contrast, in Luke 11:23, Jesus will mandate that "sitting on the fence" when it comes to Him is an impossibility. Either we are "with Him" and believe that He is our crucified and resurrected Savior and Lord, or we are "against Him." There is no middle ground. Jesus has a strong warning for those who are "lukewarm" (see Revelation 3:16).

72. Perhaps James and John were motivated by their recent visit with Elijah to punish the cruel Samaritans for their act of unkindness by destroying them by fire, much as Elijah had done centuries earlier (2 Kings 1:10–12). Jesus had not come to destroy but to save sinners, even inhospitable sinners like the Samaritans.

Later, Philip would preach the Gospel in Samaria. His preaching would be accompanied with miraculous signs, including the release of the demon possessed and the healing of paralytics and others who were crippled. This would cause a great cry of joy in the city (Acts 8:4–8). This episode should teach us not to delight in the harm or destruction of sinners but to pray and work earnestly for their deliverance through the preaching of the Good News.

73. In His conversations with three men (Luke 9:57–62), Jesus points to the cost of discipleship. Material possessions, earthly cares, and family relationships must all take second place when it comes to following our Lord.

74. Truly, the entire world is a mission field, including our own communities. "The harvest is plentiful" (Luke 10:2), which means that there is more than enough work for us to do through prayer, work with our congregation's evangelism committee, personal witness, inviting friends, family members, or coworkers to Sunday worship or a Bible-study group at home, Vacation Bible School, parish school, mission support, synodical support, and so on. We should constantly pray to God for every kind of help, and most especially for willing laborers to send out to the mission field so that souls may be won for the Lord.

75. God makes abundant promises about prayer; God uses prayer and us (Second Petition of the Lord's Prayer). When we pray, "Thy kingdom come," we ask God to send His Holy Spirit, "so that by His grace we believe His holy Word and lead godly lives here in time and there in eternity" (Luther's Small Catechism).

76. Results of mission work are not always seen at once. Some missionaries have to labor many years before they gain their first convert. At other times success is rapid and great (see Acts 2:41). The seventy were overjoyed with the miraculous results of their labors. The chief reason for our happiness, however, is that our names have been written in the Lamb's Book of Life (Philippians 4:3–4). We should rejoice in all circumstances because our names will never be blotted out of this book (Revelation 3:5; see also 20:12). God has called us by name to be His own (Isaiah 43:1–3).

77. Relying on their own human reason (Luke 10 21; see also 1 Corinthians 1:18–29), many reject the message of the cross, which is for them mere "foolishness." Without God's Spirit, spiritual things cannot be discerned (2:14). We should crave the pure, spiritual milk of God's Word so that we may grow to Christian maturity (1 Peter 2:2; "milk" is used here in a positive sense, unlike 1 Corinthians 3:2 and Hebrews 5:12–14).

78. Individually, we act as Good Samaritans in a variety of ways through Christian care and support. Corporately, the Church acts as a Good Samaritan through food pantries; health clinics or screenings; disaster aid and support; homeless or abuse victim shelters; supporting unwed mothers in avoiding abortion and throughout their pregnancy; aiding in adoption; immigrant assistance or English as a second language programs; prison, hospital, HIV/AIDS, or elderly care ministries; and so on. Discuss what your congregation is doing currently, or could be doing, to be a Good Samaritan in your community.

79. It is not enough merely to know God's Word. The Law demands perfect obedience. While no person can be saved by trying to keep the Law (Romans 3:20), Jesus does enable us to live godly lives. The Gospel gives us the power to live according to the precepts of God's Law.

The Good Samaritan provided time, medical attention, lodging, food, and clothing—"Take care of him" (Luke 10:35). From this parable, we learn that we are not only to notice and pray for, but also to provide for all of our neighbor's needs, just as our Good Samaritan, Jesus Christ, does for us.

Lesson 6

Comfort and Warning

Theme verse: *And He said to them, "When you pray, say: 'Father, hallowed be Your name. Your kingdom come.'"*

Luke 11:2

Objectives

By the power of the Holy Spirit working through God's Word, we will

- Learn that consecrated service follows the faithful hearing of God's Word and that the Christian life is a life of prayer;
- Take note that believers should guard against hypocrisy and should not allow their loyalty to Jesus to be shaken;
- Rejoice that God providentially cares for us in body and soul and that we need not worry about either eternal or temporal things.

80. Luke often mentions women disciples (see 8:2; 11:27). Mary and Martha were true believers (like Lazarus, who was perhaps away for this scene). Martha meant well but did wrong in placing *serving* before *hearing*. Likewise, we should guard against putting too much stress on "Christian life and service" while neglecting hearing the Gospel. The "one thing [that] is necessary" and "the good portion" are the hearing of God's Word. Jesus will be our permanent guest in our homes as we read and study His Word. Knowing that He is always present through His Word will have an effect on what we say and do.

81. Every family should daily take time to read God's Word together and to pray. This responsibility falls first to fathers, and in their absence, mothers. Parents are charged by God to bring up their children in the fear and knowledge of the Lord (Deuteronomy 4:9; 6:7; Ephesians 6:4).

82. Allow participants to compare the Lord's Prayer found in Luke 11:2–4 and Matthew 6:9–13. We are more familiar with the version found in Matthew, along with the doxology ("For Thine is the

kingdom . . ."). Jesus' illustrations of the friend and the father show the outstanding generosity of our heavenly Father when it comes to hearing our requests and responding according to His gracious will.

83. Jesus' teaching on prayer indicates that we should boldly approach our Father with our requests (see also Hebrews 4:16). Though we may not receive the answer we desire, Jesus teaches that all of our prayers will be answered (vv. 9–10) in God's way and timing. God is our loving heavenly Father. He will give us only good gifts (vv. 11–12). According to Luke, the greatest gift is the indwelling presence of the Holy Spirit (v. 13; see Luther's explanation of the Third Article of the Apostles' Creed).

84. The Bible teaches plainly that there is a devil and describes his great power and tyranny over man. Jesus proved that He is mightier than Satan. All who believe in Jesus are delivered from Satan's kingdom (see Luther's explanation of the Second Article of the Apostles' Creed). Unbelievers may deny that there is a devil, but they are ruled by him.

85. Jonah is a type of Jesus. Jonah's preaching to the Gentile Ninevites resulted in their sincere repentance (Jonah 3). Jonah's three-day stay in the belly of the sea creature typifies Christ's stay in the tomb (Jonah 1:17; see Luke 23:54 and 24:1–8). However, Christ's resurrection is the greatest miracle (1 Corinthians 15:3–20). The sins of those in the Old Testament should serve to warn us Christians against apathy and indifference (see 1 Corinthians 10:1–12).

86. Jesus did not wash on this occasion prior to reclining at table. Washing before meals was not part of the ceremonial law but was a tradition of the elders (see Mark 7:3–4). Jesus used this as an opportunity to rebuke the self-righteous and legalistic Pharisees, who while apparently clean on the outside, were unclean in the interior of their hearts. If the heart is not regenerated and made pure by the Gospel, all outward display of piety is hypocrisy. Pharisaism is still practiced today by those making a show of religion while their hearts are cold with pride, lovelessness toward others, and rank unbelief.

87. The lawyers misled the people with their false interpretations of the Law. Instead of opening the kingdom by pointing to the Messiah, they refused to enter the kingdom themselves by faith and also prohibited others from entering by their numerous traditions and customs. Instead of repenting, the Pharisees and lawyers became angry with Jesus and sought to destroy Him (vv. 53–54).

88. In the presence of an unusually large crowd, Jesus warned His disciples and the multitude to beware of the "leaven of the Pharisees," which is hypocrisy. (See also Matthew 16:6, 11, and 12.) Here Jesus used the figure of leaven to illustrate the secret and penetrating influence of hypocrisy. All hypocrisy shall be exposed, if not here in time, then at least on the Last Day (1 Corinthians 4:5). We should be careful to avoid religious pretense and pride (see the story of Ananias and Sapphira, Acts 5:1–11).

89. Spiritual exercises such as mealtime prayers should not cease merely because we are in a public place such as a restaurant, the food court of a shopping mall, or a school cafeteria. Of course, hypocritical showiness should be avoided. But private prayer (even inaudible, with a bowed head) can serve as a public witness of our faith and provide an opportunity for sharing the hope that is within us (Colossians 1:27). When guests visit our homes, why should our prayers and Bible readings cease? We should not be tempted to neglect God's Word and prayer for fear of embarrassment.

90. The man's personal affairs, and not the teachings of Jesus, were most important to him. He evidently believed that Jesus, with His authority and influence, could help him to earthly gain. Jesus showed that He was not interested in the case; it was no concern of His. The Jews had judges and courts for such disputes about property (separation of Church and State). Therefore Jesus warns His Church against greed or covetousness. Jesus' ministry, and likewise the ministry of His Church, is not about securing an abundance of material resources (see Ninth and Tenth Commandments; 1 Timothy 6:6–10).

91. Note how many times the rich man in the parable refers to "I" or "my." He was a fool because he was thankless toward God and paid no attention to the needs of others. He thought only of the personal enjoyment of his wealth, which was his true god. There are those like him today (1 Corinthians 15:31–32). When God delivers His verdict in verse 20, the day of grace comes swiftly to an end. It is better to be poor in material possessions and rich in God, having the forgiveness of sins and the treasures of eternal life through faith in Christ Jesus (see also Matthew 6:19–21).

92. Jesus teaches this lesson against worry also in the Sermon on the Mount (Matthew 6:25–34). Our hearts are not to be filled with anxious cares. God can and does provide food and clothing. He who gives life and body will certainly sustain both. Having a care for basic necessities is certainly different than anxiously worrying over them. To

worry means to doubt God's perfect will and promises—it is a sin; it is of the pagan world (Luke 12:30; see Matthew 6:32). The Bible contains many examples of God's providential care, and most Christians can relate experiences in their own lives when God miraculously provided for them. The Fourth Petition of the Lord's Prayer, "Give us this day our daily bread," when prayed in faith, will help us against worrying. Jesus promises to supply all the earthly needs of those who seek first His kingdom (Luke 12:31; Matthew 6:33).

93. While it is a sin to worry, it is not wrong to work, to save, and to provide for the future. Scripture has numerous passages commending hard work, thrift, and good stewardship of the material resources God bestows upon us (see Genesis 2:15; 1 Thessalonians 4:11–12; and Luke 10:7), as well as passages warning against laziness and sloth (Proverbs 10:4; 12:24; 2 Thessalonians 3:6–13).

94. In John 10:11–18, Jesus says that His sheep know Him and know His voice. Just as sheep recognize the call of their shepherd, believers recognize Jesus speaking to them through His Word. No one can snatch His sheep out of the hand of Good Shepherd Jesus (vv. 27–29). This comforts us during the most difficult trials of life.

95. Jesus has bestowed many spiritual blessings upon us, granted us a knowledge of His Word, and made us stewards of the rich treasures of His Gospel. He leaves us in this world so that we can grow in faith, bring the Gospel to other people, and keep ourselves ready for His coming.

Lesson 7

God's Power to Save

Theme verse: *And the master said to the servant, "Go out to the highways and hedges and compel people to come in, that my house may be filled."*

Luke 14:23

Objectives

By the power of the Holy Spirit working through God's Word, we will

- Learn that all troubles in the world are admonitions to repentance and that God mercifully extends His time of grace;
- Ponder that if the heart is ruled by pride and selfishness, a person cannot produce the fruits of faith;
- Rejoice that God wants all people to hear and believe the Gospel, and His disciples faithfully to use His means of grace.

96. When we are tempted to sin we should remember the extreme suffering of our Lord, which included His soul's dread of the experience (see Luke 22:41–44; see also Matthew 26:38–39; Mark 14:33–36). We are enabled to resist temptation by knowing that through His suffering Christ has conquered the world, the devil, and our sinful flesh (see Isaiah 53:5). In the midst of temptation, we recall that Christ has rescued us fully (Romans 7:21–25).

97. Jesus' ministry is one of reconciling the world to the Father and reconciling us to each other. We reconcile with each other by mutually confessing our sins to one another and pronouncing absolution, that is, offering our forgiveness for the sake of Jesus Christ, who Himself has forgiven us. We should quickly seek to be reconciled with any brother or sister, taking the initiative to admit our own faults and to offer forgiveness to those who have offended us (Fifth Petition of the Lord's Prayer). Unwillingness to forgive on our part compels God to withdraw His pardon of our sins.

98. The Galileans resisted the Roman yoke. Probably they offended Pilate by causing a demonstration in the temple. For this, he took cruel revenge. In the midst of their sacrifices, he caused them to be slain, so that their blood mingled with the sacrifices they intended to present. Jesus connects the report with a new admonition to repentance.

Some view all tragedies as the result of some especially great sins committed by the sufferers, but Jesus corrects this notion (see John 9:2–3). The sufferers were no worse than others. Jesus teaches the same lesson by referring to the collapse of a tower that killed eighteen at the Pool of Siloam, near Jerusalem (see John 9:7). Christ gives this rule: all suffering is the result of sin. This is meant to discipline believers and to lead unbelievers to repentance. God continues warning the world of the need for repentance today through terrorism, tsunamis, hurricanes, tornadoes, and so on. Christians can be of service to other people during these times by providing compassionate help and aid and by clearly proclaiming both Law and Gospel.

99. The parable of the unfruitful fig tree points to God's efforts in securing repentance from His people. Israel received God's grace for a period of time but did not produce the fruit of sincere repentance. The vinedresser bestowing special care on the fig tree in the fourth year signifies the coming of Christ. If the people allow this last period to pass by unimproved, the fig tree will be cast away and the kingdom of God will be taken from it. Christ did not come to condemn, but to restore us to the Father (Romans 8:34). He is our advocate before Him (1 John 2:1–2). We should daily take advantage of this "fourth year" through repentance and faith in our Savior.

100. God allowed Satan ("a disabling spirit" [v. 11]; "whom Satan bound" [v. 16]) to burden the woman with this physical infirmity. She is healed by Jesus' Word accompanied by His touch, symbolic of His healing power. The woman's faith proved that she was a true spiritual descendent of Abraham (Romans 4:16) and expressed itself through her heartfelt praises to God (v. 13; see Hebrews 11). By not participating in the means of grace, we neither hear Christ's life-giving Word nor receive His touch of spiritual healing, which comes only through Word and Sacrament.

101. The ruler of the synagogue was angry because the miracle was performed on a Sabbath. He showed cowardice in scolding the people when his true target was Jesus. Jesus rebuked him with piercing words. The Talmud had minute rules for leading out animals on the Sabbath. The hypocrites pretended their zeal for the Sabbath was the

result of their zeal for God. But Jesus' actions showed that the relief of human sorrow and suffering is always in season. We should never become like the synagogue ruler: indifferent to the suffering of others—especially under the pretense of "religion."

102. Rather than ascertain the number of those attaining salvation, one should be concerned about receiving salvation for oneself and others. For the benefit of all, Jesus repeated the saying in the Sermon on the Mount (Matthew 7:13–14). There is only one gate to eternal life; Jesus is the only door (John 10:9; 14:6; Hebrews 10:19–20). The only way to enter this door is by faith. Those who presume to get to heaven by their own works, reason, or religious experiences are fooling themselves. Condemnation comes only through unbelief (Mark 16:16).

103. External acquaintance with Jesus and outward membership in the congregation are no passports to heaven. The parable of the ten virgins (Matthew 25:1–13) serves to warn against casual indifference to the Lord's coming; we are to remain prepared through repentance and faith. We best prepare for His return by confessing our sins, making use of the means of grace, and living lives worthy of our heavenly calling. Those who in patent unbelief do not do so—regardless if they are listed on a congregation's membership roster—will be among those who weep and gnash their teeth on the Last Day (Luke 13:28–30).

104. Jesus earnestly tries to save even those who reject His grace. Jerusalem was the murderess of her prophets. In Amos 7:10–13, Amaziah, who served the king in Bethel, rejects Amos's ministry and seeks to return him to Judah for faithfully prophesying God's Word. When the high priest and the Sadducees were irritated by the preaching of Peter and the other apostles, they brought them before the Sanhedrin to silence them. Peter and his fellow preachers replied, "We must obey God rather than men" (Acts 5:29).

105. The word picture Jesus provides is of a mother hen reaching out with her wings to draw her chicks to herself to protect them. This is a powerful image of the desire and work of our Savior to draw His people to Himself. God doesn't want the wicked to die in unbelief (Ezekiel 33:11); rather, He wants all to be saved and to know the truth (1 Timothy 2:4), repenting of their sins and believing in His Son (2 Peter 3:9).

106. Jesus does not use this occasion to show how to gain honor in a clever way by taking the worst seat to acquire a better one. The

parable does not sanction sham humility but sets forth genuine humility. The key to the parable is verse 11. Pharisaic pride and self-glorification will be abased, cast down. Genuine humility, on the other hand, is a fruit of repentance and faith. Paul reminds us of the ultimate humility expressed by our Savior (Philippians 2:5–11).

107. Ultimately, Jesus' words here teach that we are not to forget charity. The believer will easily find ways and means of helping the needy and will not think of his or her own advantages. God promises that He will graciously reward our good works, even though they deserve no recognition (see Matthew 25:34–40).

108. In this parable, Jesus speaks about the kingdom of grace, typified by the great banquet. The invitation to the banquet is the message of the Gospel, proclaimed by the prophets, John, Jesus, the apostles, and Christian pastors. The excuses are personal interests: property, business transactions, pleasure. The parable shows that God's grace is by "invitation only," first to the nation of Israel (those making excuses; see Romans 3:2; 9:5), then to us ("the poor, the crippled, the lame, the blind" [v. 13]). The invitation to God's grace through the Gospel is not based on human merit or worthiness; it invites all, regardless of race, class, gender or other distinctions, to the feast.

109. The use of banquet imagery as an occasion of joyful feasting should motivate us toward evangelism and mission work. Everyone is invited to the feast of God's grace in Christ! As the parable says, "Go out quickly to the streets and lanes of the city, and bring in . . ." (v. 21). Whether small or great, our labors for the Lord will provide results (1 Corinthians 15:58).

110. Our love of Christ must come before all other love, including love for family members. Discipleship is like building a house and waging a war. One must not only joyfully intend, but also carefully consider, firmly resolve, follow it through, and carry it out. Only divine grace will take us through. The Gospel gives us the means to build our spiritual lives and the strength to overcome our spiritual enemies (Ephesians 6:13–20). With Christ on our side, victory is certain (see 2 Kings 6:16; Romans 8:31). Church members who expect ease and rely on themselves do not "count the cost."

111. Christians are good salt when they show the quality and character of true discipleship. They should be sincere in their confession and in their service. Otherwise, they are worthless; they cannot purify and season the world.

Lesson 8

"Jesus Sinners Doth Receive"

Theme verse: *"For this my son was dead, and is alive again; he was lost, and is found." And they began to celebrate.*

Luke 15:24

Objectives

By the power of the Holy Spirit working through God's Word, we will

- Give thanks that the glorious work of Jesus and His Church is to seek lost sinners and bring them into His kingdom;
- Learn that God freely forgives all who confess their sins and accept His pardon in Christ;
- Ponder that God has made us His stewards on earth and will someday require us to give an account of our stewardship.

112. This parable about the lost sheep (the first of three about something that is lost) shows us not only the value God places on us individually, but also to what extent God goes, through His Son, Jesus Christ, to find us. Luke's consistent theme of joy experienced at conversion ("joy in heaven" [v. 7]) figures here. We are like sheep when we wander (Isaiah 53:6), but Jesus is our "Shepherd and Overseer" (1 Peter 2:25) who attends to all of His sheep (John 10:16).

113. The parable of the lost coin is similar to the previous one, but it has a slight difference. The coin could not lose itself; it occurred in the woman's house owing to carelessness or an accident. Therefore, we cannot identify the woman with Christ. Luther says, "This parable of the woman deals with the Christian Church, which holds the office of the holy ministry to this purpose, that the poor sinners may be called to repentance, and may be saved from eternal death and damnation." The Church should look for the indifferent and erring. The lamp is God's Word, which lays bare hearts. Individual believers, too, through

their prayers and support of the Church's ministry, seek to win back those who have fallen away.

114. In relation to the two parables preceding it, the parable of the lost son, or even lost sons, shows the experience of all those living a life of sin. Sin separates from God, destroys spiritual life, and ruins body and soul. The sinner cannot find his or her way back to God; God works repentance and faith through His Word.

115. God is wonderful in His love and grace through Jesus Christ. When we return to Him in repentance, He says, "Let us eat and celebrate" (Luke 15:23). While the younger son imagined returning to his father as a hired worker (v. 19), the father accepted his son without any "works" at all. The lost son "was dead, and is alive; he was lost, and is found" (v. 32). The radical nature of salvation (dead/alive; lost/found) through Jesus Christ is by God's grace, through faith in Christ, without our works.

116. Though he was in his father's house, the older brother was lost too. By including the older brother in the parable, Christ entreats the Pharisees to forsake their self-righteousness. God's kingdom is one of divine grace, love, and mercy. God seeks to rescue all lost sinners. One may be a churchgoer and still be outside the kingdom. What the older brother did to answer his father's appeal, we are not told. This portion of the parable warns us not to despise the grace of God.

117. The elder brother may not have loved his father, he proudly boasted of his virtues, and he was resentful of his work. In their words and deeds, the self-righteous prove that they, too, are sinners. Believers should think like Paul (1 Timothy 1:15) and Job (Job 42:6).

118–119. Allow participants time to discuss these questions.

120. In the parable of the shrewd manager, Jesus teaches that we do not have an absolute right to do whatever we please with our earthly possessions. All things belong to God, including the world and everything in it—even our bodies and souls. God entrusts us to be good stewards of all that He gives us both materially (1 Peter 4:10) and spiritually (see 1 Corinthians 4:1). As Christians, we should use our resources for God's glory and the good of our fellow people.

121. Everything we have we hold in trust and will have to give an account for on Judgment Day. We should be faithful in our use of earthly blessings. God wants us to use our life, money, talents, time, and so on for the good of other people. Faith's fruit, including the use of what He entrusted to us during this life, will be graciously rewarded

in heaven. The parable clarifies for us the importance of supporting God's work through the Church.

122. Some people try in vain to serve both God and Mammon, material possessions. The Pharisees were not acceptable to God because they "were lovers of money" (v. 14). Wealth is not the main thing in life. There is a danger of rating it too highly and becoming its slave. Each person will attach his or her heart to some treasure. If this treasure is something in this life, it will not be God and the heavenly treasures. People ruled by the love of money cannot serve God. They are severely tempted, end up ruined, and lose their faith (see 1 Timothy 6:9–10).

123. We might try to serve both God and money by putting a greater emphasis on material possessions than we do on service to God. Left unchecked, we can develop patterns of spending and incur indebtedness that cause unrelenting grief. We can prevent Mammon from ruling over us by confessing to the Lord our idolatry of money and possessions and by receiving His forgiveness through His means of grace. Disciplining ourselves by following a reasonable budget that includes necessary expenditures, savings, and regular contributions to the Church will put the desire for material things into perspective.

124. The rich man was not condemned because of his wealth; nor was Lazarus saved because of his poverty. Rather, the rich man showed his lack of faith by his actions. Lazarus had faith (Lazarus means "God is help") and, in spite of his lack of financial or material resources, was comforted with the hope that awaited him (Luke 16:25; see Romans 8:18). The rich man should have learned repentance through God's goodness to him, but he failed this lesson (Romans 2:4). He serves as a warning to those who have been blessed with wealth not to put their trust in it. Abraham, a rich man himself, did not trust in his material possessions, but in the promises of God (Genesis 15:6; see also Romans 4:11; Hebrews 11:8).

125. It is foolish to imagine that there is not a literal hell, a place of everlasting torment for unbelievers, as this story and other passages of Scripture teach (see also Matthew 8:12; Revelation 20:10; 14:11). Fire, agony, and separation are depicted here. Isaiah envisions unspeakable, everlasting torment for resurrected unbelievers in both body and soul (Isaiah 66:24), which is likewise affirmed by Jesus (Mark 9:43–48). We should prepare for eternity now through repentance and faith in Jesus as our only Savior from sin, death, and hell (2 Corinthians 6:2).

Lesson 9

Disciples Pray for Increase of Faith

Theme Verse: *But Jesus called them to Him, saying, "Let the children come to me, and do not hinder them, for to such belongs the kingdom of God."*

Luke 18:16

Objectives

By the power of the Holy Spirit working through God's Word, we will

- Affirm that just as God forgives us richly in Christ, we should always be willing to forgive when we have been offended;
- Rejoice that while the kingdom of God remains hidden now, it will be revealed on the Last Day;
- Give thanks for God's help that encourages us to continue to pray with perseverance and firm confidence.

126. Instead of giving others occasion to sin, Christians should help them to forsake sin. A brother or sister who has given offense (offended us or others) should be admonished (see Matthew 18:15–17). Even believers may fall into a grievous sin (1 Corinthians 10:12). The aim of rebuke is that the sinner may repent (Luke 3:3). By refusing to forgive someone who has sinned against us, we show that we do not desire the Lord's forgiveness (see Matthew 18:35; James 2:13).

127. Even if believers could do their duty fully, they would nevertheless in the sight of God be undeserving, "unworthy servants" (Luke 17:10). It is better that we say this in true humility than God say it about us (Matthew 25:30). God not only graciously rewards faithful servants but even those who have not fully succeeded in doing "what was commanded" (see Luke 17:9; 19:17; Matthew 19:21; 25:21).

128. The lepers stood at a distance, as they dared not approach anyone. Jesus only said that they should go to the priests in Jerusalem. The lepers knew the significance of this command; they would receive a legal attestation (as from a Department of Health) of their cure, be reinstated in society, and bring God a thank offering (Leviticus 13:2, 17; 14:2; see also Luke 5:14). God uses adversity as an opportunity for repentance and the strengthening of faith. As such, the illness may be seen as a spiritual blessing under the guise of physical suffering. Though we should call upon God in every trouble (Psalm 50:15), those who call on God only when they are in trouble exhibit a weak faith.

129. Only the Samaritan returned to offer Jesus thanks. The former leper had time to see the priest and receive an attestation of his healing later. He did not return in vain (v. 19); Jesus strengthened him and graciously rewarded his faith (see Psalm 118:1). Lack of gratitude to God exhibits a lack of faith. Because God gives us all things for this life (see the First Article of the Apostles' Creed), we should daily give Him thanks for all things.

130. The Jews refused to acknowledge Jesus as the Messiah. They were looking for an earthly kingdom, a realm of outward glory. Jesus shows that they have no conception of what God's kingdom is like. It has been present on earth all along. We recognize the presence of Christ's kingdom of grace through His Word (Isaiah 55:11) and Sacraments. We know that we are part of His kingdom through faith in God's Son (Ephesians 2:8–9; Romans 8:15–17).

131. Jesus' return will be sudden, swift, and final. Believers should not be deceived by the talk of "two comings" (the false rapture theory) taught by the millennialists. It will be a day of judgment for unbelievers and a day of rejoicing for believers. We must not look back, that is, have an attachment of heart to earthly things, as Lot's wife did for Sodom. Those who imitate her conduct today are concerned only with preserving earthly life and temporal goods. They will lose both these and eternal life (Matthew 10:39).

132. Till the end, the disciples must always keep praying and never lose heart. How much more gracious and responsive is our heavenly Father than the unrighteous judge! He is a true friend (Luke 11:5–8)! Even when we in our prayers "wrestle" with Him as Jacob did (Genesis 32:24–30), He hears and answers according to His will (see Psalm 35:17; 74:10; 94:3; Revelation 6:10).

133. Paul imitated the example of the publican (v. 13) by approaching God in prayer with humility (1 Timothy 1:15). We

approach God's throne of grace with confidence only because of the blood of Christ, who has atoned for our sins (Hebrews 4:16; 10:19–20).

134. Luke speaks about "infants," who were too small to know what was being done for them. Jesus rebuked His disciples for their interference. He does not imply that infants are innocent and sinless (see Genesis 5:3; Psalm 51:5; John 3:6). If infants had no sin, there would be no need for them to be brought to Christ. In their unassuming humility and unquestioning trustfulness and receptivity, they are the patterns for adults (see Psalm 131). All must have such a simple and trustful faith to enter Christ's kingdom. Parents keep their children from Jesus by not having them baptized, not reading Bible stories to them and praying with them, and not bringing them to public worship and Sunday School. Infants should be baptized because all people are conceived and born sinful (Psalm 51:5) and because Baptism saves (1 Peter 3:21). The refusal to baptize infants is a denial of both original sin and baptismal regeneration.

135. Jesus would have been pleased with the young man if he had combined a believing heart with his piety. Some young people lack even his sincerity and earnestness. It is important to free the heart from worldly attractions (1 John 2:15–17). Because Jesus loves young people, He asks them to sacrifice the things that would draw their hearts from Him. No one is saved by works—even giving away all their riches to the poor. Salvation is by God's grace through faith in Christ, not by works (Ephesians 2:8–9).

136. Neither rich nor poor can have faith as long as they trust in riches. God's Word alone can break the power of Mammon, which is an idol. Paul warns about the dire consequences of the desire to become wealthy and falling in love with money (1 Timothy 6:9–10). Some versions of the Bible have "for those who trust in riches" in Mark 10:24. The point is not the abundance or lack of wealth, it is faith. Is our faith in God's grace through Christ? Or do we trust in riches? Both rich and poor can make an idol of money.

137. We should not regret any sacrifice of time, talent, treasure, or position because of Christ and His Church. We will be rewarded (Luke 18:29–30). In spite of our outward circumstances, due to Christ's poverty we have become rich (2 Corinthians 8:9).

Lesson 10

The King Seeks Subjects

Theme verse: *For the Son of Man came to seek and to save the lost.*

Luke 19:10

Objectives

By the power of the Holy Spirit working through God's Word, we will

- Affirm that the Gospel is the greatest treasure that God has committed to our stewardship and that faithful use of it will be graciously rewarded;
- Learn that God is patient with impenitent sinners, but if they continue to reject the Gospel, He will take it from them and punish them for their unbelief;
- Understand that obedience to God includes submission to all lawful human authority for His sake.

138. This familiar story may be used as a contrast to Luke 18:18–27. Zacchaeus was a rich man who learned how he could become rich in God (see 12:21; 1 Timothy 6:17–19). Zacchaeus was not merely curious about Jesus, as the context proves. Rather, he was in spiritual distress and yearned to see Jesus. He had heard that Jesus was the "Friend of tax collectors and sinners" (Luke 7:34). Jesus didn't accidentally discover him in the tree (v. 5). He knew the man's name and read his heart (see John 1:43–50; 2:24–25). Jesus pointed to Zacchaeus's faith by calling him a "son of Abraham" (v. 9). His faith expressed itself in concern for the poor and restitution for those whom he had wronged (v. 8).

139. It is not money or wealth that is evil; it is the desires of the heart concerning money or wealth that may be evil. Jesus didn't demand that Zacchaeus sell everything and give it to the poor as He had the rich young ruler (Luke 18:22) because Zacchaeus had repented of this idolatry and trusted in Him. His willingness to make amends

through charity and restitution were the fruits of his faith. Every believer follows Zacchaeus's example through repentance and faith, which lead to sanctification of life (Ephesians 2:10).

140. This parable is not the same as the parable of the talents found in Matthew 25:14–30. In this parable the "nobleman" is Jesus, the "far country" is heaven, and the ten "servants" are His disciples. "Ten" symbolizes completeness. The Gospel is an investment given to the Church for doing the King's spiritual business in the world. The "mina" gets all the credit (Psalm 115:1; 1 Corinthians 1:31); the Word has done it all. Jesus is concerned about the use we make of the Gospel for the sake of the world (John 3:16).

141. All work for the Lord will be rewarded. The highest honors in heaven will go to the most faithful. Those who are able to bring only a smaller return (the second servant) from their use of God's Word will also receive a reward of grace. The second servant is described for the comfort of weaker Christians, but all should strive to be as faithful as the first, not for the sake of greater glory, but from love for our Savior. The worst that a professed Christian can do with the Gospel is to make no use of it, either for self or for others.

142. This passage will recall to mind both the liturgy for Palm Sunday and the closing portion of the Sanctus from the Divine Service: "Blessed is He who comes in the name of the Lord." Luke omits the waving of palm branches but recalls that the people also sang a phrase ("Peace in heaven and glory in the highest!") similar to Luke 2:14. The crowd spread their cloaks below the colt that was carrying Jesus. This act of submission is combined with the highest honor. We show our loyalty to Jesus as our King by confessing our sins, trusting in His mercy, and resolving with His help to live according to His will (Third Petition of the Lord's Prayer).

143. The crowd turned from praise to scorn with shouts of "Crucify, crucify Him!" on Good Friday (Luke 23:21). The same thing happens today when some sing praises to Christ and then crucify Him afresh by rejecting Him (see Hebrews 6:6).

144. Scripture records Jesus' weeping following the death of His friend, Mary and Martha's brother, Lazarus (John 11:35). By exhibiting normal, healthy emotions, Jesus indicated His full humanity. Here, His sorrow was expressed in loud sobbing, showing how the attitude of Jerusalem affected His divine heart. He saw the true condition of the city and how judgment would descend upon it (see Luke 13:34–35; Matthew 24:1–2).

145. In AD 70, the Roman general Titus built a palisaded wall, or rampart, around Jerusalem and finally destroyed and burned the city and the temple; over one million Jews were killed. We should make the most of every opportunity to receive God's grace through the Gospel (2 Corinthians 6:2).

146. Having cleansed the temple a second time (Monday of Passion Week; Luke 19:45–47), Jesus returned the next morning. In the parable of the tenants, the wicked tenants are the rulers, priests, and teachers of the people. They have beaten and thrown out the prophets ("servants"). They will crucify ("kill") Jesus ("son") outside of the city ("out of the vineyard"). The wicked tenants today are heterodox churches, pastors, and teachers who do not teach God's Word but the word of man. They are known by their fruits: the effect their preaching and teaching has on their hearers (Matthew 7:15–20; see also 1 Timothy 6:3–5; 2 Peter 2).

147. This parable should serve as a warning for all Christians of the dangers of false doctrine from religious leaders whose teachings ultimately destroy faith (Romans 11:20–22).

148. A believer recognizes all governments as instituted by God for the preservation and welfare of a civil society. Those who rebel against the civil government rebel against God, who established it (Romans 13). Christ affirms God's "left-hand" rule (civil authority; Luke 20:25). The State should support but not interfere in churchly affairs; likewise the Church should support the State but not interfere in civil affairs. This does not mean, however, that individual members of the Church, who are citizens of the State, should not take an active role in civil government, speak to issues of morality, or promote the general welfare of the society as a whole. Citizenship is a godly vocation and, like all vocations, should be exercised in faith and in accordance with God's Word.

149. Like the apostles, Christians must "obey God rather than men" when civil laws violate God's Word (Acts 5:29).

150. Unlike the Pharisees who affirmed these beliefs, the Sadducees denied both the existence of angelic beings and a general resurrection of the dead. Jesus' clear words about the resurrection and the state of couples who were married in this life refute the Sadducees' arguments without falling into their trap. Immediately upon death, the souls of believers enter into the heavenly presence of Christ and all the saints who have preceded them (Luke 23:43; see also Ecclesiastes 12:7; John 17:24; Philippians 1:23–24; Revelation 14:13).

151. The teaching of the resurrection of Christ from the dead is an essential part of the Christian faith and message. We are saved by Christ's life, death, and resurrection. We are baptized into Christ's death and resurrection (Romans 6:3–4).

152. Jesus' question in verse 44 addresses the mystery of a son of David, literally the Son of David, also being David's Lord. This question drives at the very identity of the Messiah: He is both David's Lord, that is, God, and David's Son, that is, man. The only solution to the apparent problem, and the only correct answer to this question, is that the Messiah is *both* God *and* man (see Peter's confession in Matthew 16:16 and John 6:68–69).

153. The scribes enjoyed the glory of being honored by the people. People bowed to them and offered them the most prominent seats at banquets. To love of glory they added selfishness, which even did not hesitate to rob the poor. Because they could quote Scripture (which even Satan does, see Luke 4), they were often entrusted with the guardianship of estates. They used long prayers as a veil for their greed. Because of the hypocritical show of religion, they would receive "greater condemnation" (v. 47). Christians should beware of religious leaders, pastors, and teachers who exhibit a love of power and money (see 1 Timothy 3:1–7; Titus 1:5–9).

Lesson 11

Our Passover Lamb

Theme Verse: *And He took bread, and when He had given thanks, He broke it and gave it to them, saying, "This is My body, which is given for you. Do this in remembrance of Me." And likewise the cup after they had eaten, saying, "This cup that is poured out for you is the new covenant in My blood."*

Luke 22:19–20

Objectives

By the power of the Holy Spirit working through God's Word, we will

- Resolve to patiently bear our crosses for Jesus' sake, remain steadfast in the faith, and be constantly prepared to meet Jesus;
- Rejoice that Jesus willingly sacrificed Himself to save the world and that in the Lord's Supper He offers us the benefits of His suffering and death;
- Give thanks that Jesus constantly prays for us and wants us to use prayer as a means to guard against temptation.

154. Jesus reads our hearts and is concerned chiefly about the spirit in which we give to Him. Christian giving is both deliberate and proportionate (1 Corinthians 16:2). What we return to the Lord is to be done cheerfully; otherwise our gifts are made under compulsion, which does not please God (2 Corinthians 9:6–7). God blesses us by giving us all of our gifts and blesses others through us as we give gifts to them (vv. 8–9). God's giving to us is proportionate to our good stewardship; the more we give in faith, the more He will entrust into our care (vv. 10–11). Ultimately, others are blessed through our giving by receiving the ultimate gift, Jesus Christ (vv. 12–15).

155. The poor widow gave all she had in faith (two copper coins, or mites). Hers was a real sacrifice; she gave all that she had, whereas the rich gave of their excess. Jesus establishes the principle by which

gifts are to be valued in the Church—like prayer, worship, or other spiritual exercises. Giving is an exercise of faith. Thus, even the poor should give deliberately and proportionately as God provides the means to do so.

156. Wars, earthquakes, famine, and a variety of natural disasters all warn unbelievers to repent and encourage believers to place their hope in the return of Christ. No amount of tribulation can shake the faith of God's elect. Those who claim to know the date and time of Christ's coming should be avoided as false prophets and teachers. Their predictions will always fail because the Lord has chosen not to reveal the date and time of the Last Day.

157. Allow participants to recall examples. War and disaster are constant. There will never be an era of perfect international peace apart from the restoration of all creation brought about by the Son of Man on the Last Day. The thousand-year kingdom of Christ is now: the time of the Church. Millennialists err in teaching that Christ will first return for a secret rapture and then return again to establish a millennial kingdom.

158. The destruction of Jerusalem in AD 70, which Christ prophesied in verses 20–24, should teach us to always be alert and ready for His return, which will be preceded by international distresses and natural disasters (vv. 25–26). Christians should constantly be watching for the return of our precious Savior as our mighty King. How we will rejoice when we see our Redeemer face-to-face (vv. 27–28; see Job 19:25–27)!

159. Peter (2 Peter 3:10–12) describes the Last Day (the "day of the Lord") as coming quickly and without warning ("like a thief"). The entire universe will be transformed. Observable changes in the heavens and the earth will be made (Joel 2:30–31). Christ will come as the exalted Son of Man (Revelation 1:13–17; 6:16). All people will see Him in His divine majesty, on the clouds (Daniel 7:13; Acts 1:9, 11), with His omnipotent power and in radiant glory (John 17:5; 2 Thessalonians 1:7; 1 Peter 1:7; 4:13; Philippians 2:10–11).

160. In the context of the Last Day, "redemption" is the final deliverance from evil. Judgment Day is not an occasion for fear by believers; it is a day of rejoicing (Romans 8:21; Isaiah 35:10; 1 Thessalonians 1:5–10). "Raise your heads" is an indication of joy and hope. "The fig tree and all the trees" show seasonal changes through their foliage. (When Jesus spoke this parable, Easter was near.) Believers have certain tokens of Christ's coming. "This generation" refers to the Jewish people. Their continuation as a people reminds us

of this prophecy. Only God's Word will remain forever without change (John 14:6; Matthew 5:18; Isaiah 40:8; Psalm 119:89).

161. Believers can make the study of nature, of history, and of world events profitable for their spiritual life, judging all things in the light of God's Word. We should guard against the sins of the flesh (v. 34), which dull the senses and destroy faith. The cares of life weigh upon the soul and cause it to distrust God. Because the Last Day will come suddenly and unexpectedly, it is necessary daily to heed and follow Christ's admonition (v. 36; see also Mark 13:32–37).

162. The Passover, a one-day festival, began that year on Thursday evening. The Feast of Unleavened Bread began on Friday and lasted seven days. The two festivals were combined, and their names are used interchangeably. Passover means the Passover lamb (see Exodus 12). The lambs were slaughtered by the priest in the temple court on Thursday afternoon. Christ, our Passover Lamb (1 Corinthians 5:7), was sacrificed on a cross outside the city (Hebrews 13:11–14). Just as the Jews ate the flesh of their sacrificed Passover lambs (which pointed to Christ), so we in the Lord's Supper eat the flesh and drink the blood (1 Corinthians 10:16) of the Lamb of God, who takes away the world's sins (John 1:29).

163. The solemnity of the occasion (the Passover meal, Jesus' last will and testament, the night of His betrayal and arrest) affirms a literal reading of the text. Jesus, our Lord, does not lie. His words impart what they mean. Jesus gives us His true body and His true blood in the Sacrament of the Altar for the forgiveness of our sins, life, and salvation (Small Catechism, "The Sacrament of the Altar"). "For you" (vv. 19–20) implies our participation in the Sacrament, which provides the forgiveness of sins. Faith draws us to partake of it frequently.

164. No servants being present, who would serve whom became an issue for the disciples. That is a pagan notion. Jesus refers to His own example (John 13). The disciples would be sifted like wheat (see Job 1), that is, put through severe trials. Headstrong Peter would get into danger through his own fault. But Jesus would pray for them (and for us). We should be constantly on guard against Satan, who would also "sift" (v. 31) us. When our brothers or sisters fall into sin, we should seek to restore them through admonishment and forgiveness.

165. Believers should not despair when they sin but should repent, trusting solely in the merits of Christ. Christ has not only atoned for the sins of the world—including all of our sins, past, present, and future—He is also our Advocate, speaking our defense,

before the Father (1 John 2:1–2). He is our High Priest, who makes constant intercession for us before God's throne (Hebrews 7:25).

166. Luke alone mentions the angel and Christ's bloody sweat. Jesus' prayer in the garden teaches us about the importance of praying sincerely and humbly. Sending the angel was the Father's answer to His prayers. His human nature needed strength for the ordeal. Needing strength ourselves, we should approach our heavenly Father in the name of Christ, seeking help and comfort during our trials and distresses. The value of prayer is tremendous. God does not need our prayers; we need them.

167. Jesus expressed His love for His enemies by the way He treated His betrayer and His captors. John records that it was Simon Peter who cut off the right ear of the high priest's servant, Malchus (John 18:10). Jesus will have no part in the violence at His arrest; He heals the servant's ear (v. 51).

168. All of the evangelists record Peter's denial (see Matthew 26:69–75; Mark 14:66–72; John 18:15–18, 25–27). Peter fell in an hour of weakness and not by deliberately planning a sinful act like Judas. Jesus tries to help sinners rise again. The story of Peter is valuable to all believers because if Peter can be restored by God's grace in Christ, all of us can be restored following our fall into sin.

Allow participants to discuss situations in which a denial of the Christian faith might happen.

169. Peter's repentance comforts us because true repentance is a fruit of faith. It is a model for us. Jesus' direct gaze reminded Peter of Jesus' words about his denial of the divine Son of God, whom Peter had earlier confessed (Luke 9:20). We see Jesus and receive His pardon in His Word and Sacraments.

Lesson 12

Our Triumphant Savior

Theme verse: *While He blessed them, He parted from them and was carried up into heaven. And they worshiped Him and returned to Jerusalem with great joy, and were continually in the temple blessing God.*

Luke 24:51–53

Objectives

By the power of the Holy Spirit working through God's Word, we will

- Give thanks that by His willing and patient suffering, Jesus revealed His great love for sinners;
- Affirm that Christ's resurrection is the firm basis for our faith and that this biblical truth can clear away all doubts, fear, and sadness from our hearts;
- Be assured by Christ's ascension to God's right hand of His powerful presence among us in His means of grace and of His return to take us to be with Him forever.

170. Here it will be helpful to read John 18:28–32 after verse 2. They could not bring the charge of blasphemy before Pilate because he would have ridiculed them. Instead, they brought three false charges: (1) Jesus stirred up the people to rebel against the Romans. But Jesus had taught the people to respect and obey the government. (2) He forbade the people to pay taxes to the Romans. But Jesus Himself paid taxes (Matthew 17:24–27; see 22:21). (3) He claimed to be a king. But He was no rival of Caesar; His kingdom is not of this world. Pilate ignored the first two charges and looked into the third with incredulity (John 18:33–38). Although Pilate's verdict is an acquittal, he committed injustice by not immediately releasing Jesus and by shifting the responsibility to Herod and, later, to the mob.

171. Jesus' silence before Herod (Antipas, son of Herod the Great) was a rebuke. Jesus had no interest in performing tricks for this man. When Jesus was returned to Pilate, Pilate again acquitted Him. As a compromise to appease the crowd, he had Jesus flogged. But that did not satisfy them. Pilate conceded by releasing Barabbas, a robber and a murderer (Matthew 27:26). Pilate's actions show the disastrous results of shirking one's duty through fear and compromise. Jesus was declared innocent in two courts, and yet He died a criminal's death, aided by a man who lacked both courage and faith.

172. Simon from Cyrene (a city in Libya) was ordered to carry the cross—possibly just the horizontal crossbeam and not the entire Latin cross we often see portrayed in portraits and movies. Crossbeams weighed perhaps 30–40 pounds. Jesus began carrying His cross (see John 19:17) but was unable to continue due to being so severely weakened by flogging. To assist the Lord in any endeavor is a great privilege. We should daily take up our cross and follow Him (Luke 9:23) through repentance and faith.

173. The women raised the death wail customary among the Jews. Jesus does not want our pity; such tears for Him are wasted. Sentimentality is fruitless. Rather, let sinners weep like Peter (22:62). These women were not disciples but representatives of the nation. Jesus refers to God's wrath and judgment in AD 70, and childlessness for these women would not be a curse, as normally thought, but a blessing.

Jesus' enormous suffering teaches us the enormity of our sin. Verse 31 is a proverbial statement. The "green wood" is Jesus in His sinlessness; the "dry wood" is the Jews in their sinfulness, ripe for judgment. Luke relates the story of the penitent thief to show that Jesus is the compassionate Savior (as his Gospel often shows).

174. A number of miraculous events took place on Calvary: (1) The supernatural darkness from noon to 3:00 p.m. could not have been a natural eclipse because of the full moon. There was general darkness over the whole dayside of the earth; this was noticed by pagan writers. Darkness signifies judgment (Joel 2:31; 3:14–15; Isaiah 5:30; 13:9–10; Matthew 24:29; Luke 21:25). God sat in judgment over the sins of the world. The climax of Christ's agony occurred at this time (Matthew 27:46). Jesus was forsaken by God, and endured the eternal punishment of hell. (2) The inner veil of the temple was 60 × 30 feet and about 3 inches thick and hung between the Holy Place and the Holy of Holies (Exodus 26:31–33; 36:35). The Holy of Holies, hidden to the

human eye, was suddenly exposed by the tearing of the veil from top to bottom, signifying that the Old Testament sacrifices were at an end; the sinner now has direct access to God through the broken body and poured-out blood of Christ (Hebrews 9:8–22; 10:19–20).

175. The significance of Christ's death and burial are that the sins of the world have been atoned for; God has been reconciled to us through the life, death, and resurrection of His Son; God has accepted Christ's sacrifice (Romans 4:25); our justification before God has been completed; and we are assured of forgiveness, life, and salvation through faith in Him.

176. The bodily resurrection of Jesus Christ is the climax of the Gospels (see also Matthew 28:1–10; Mark 16:1–8). If Christ has not been raised bodily from the dead, our faith is in vain (1 Corinthians 15:14–20). But Christ is risen! He is risen indeed! Alleluia!

177. The great lesson of Easter is Christ's victory over sin, Satan, death, and hell won for us. Easter proclaims our redemption and that we now belong to Christ; heaven is opened, and we shall arise from the dead (see Job 19:25–27; Romans 4:23–25; 1 Corinthians 15:19–24, 53–57). The proofs of Christ's resurrection include the numerous eyewitness accounts recorded in the Scriptures, the apostolic preaching based on the resurrection and recorded in the Scriptures, and the internal witness of the Holy Spirit in our hearts.

178. The only means by which God brings a person to faith and sustains it is through the means of grace, that is, the Gospel preached or written, and the Sacraments. Christ's speaking to the two men on the road centered upon Himself as presented in the Scriptures: the Gospel in the Old Testament (Luke 24:25–27; see also vv. 44–47).

179. Jesus consistently affirms the value the Old Testament has for us by explaining "in all the Scriptures the things concerning Himself" (v. 27).

180. This was only one of the many appearances by Jesus following His resurrection, but it was the first to the whole group of disciples (Thomas excluded; see John 20:24–29). Jesus had already appeared to Mary Magdalene, the other women, Peter, and the Emmaus disciples. For the later ones, see John 20–21; 1 Corinthians 15:6–7. Note again that the instruction from God's Word wrought the change in the disciples.

181. Jesus' bodily appearance was sudden and miraculous. His glorified body is not confined to time and space. Jesus gives evidence of His bodily resurrection by showing His hands and feet (John adds,

“His side”). They could see His wounds and feel His flesh. Jesus gives another bodily proof by eating before the disciples, not to sustain His body, but to show that it was His own physical body (see Genesis 18:6–8; 19:3). Jesus’ resurrected body, while physical and natural, is able to do remarkable, supernatural things. God’s promise is that our resurrected bodies will be like Jesus’ body (Philippians 3:21).

182. Luke ends his Gospel as he began: with a note of joyful praise. Having opened the apostles’ minds through the Scriptures concerning Himself, Jesus commissions them as His witnesses to all nations, but only after the promised outpouring of the Holy Spirit (vv. 44–49). Christ’s ascension was prophesied in the Old Testament (Psalm 47:5–8; 68:18) as a glorious event. Elijah had ascended bodily into heaven (2 Kings 2:11), as did Enoch (Genesis 5:24).

183. Luke notes the joy, praise, blessing, and continuous worship of the disciples. Christ’s ascension pertains only to His human nature. It was both His coronation and exaltation (Daniel 7:13–14; Psalm 110:1; Hebrews 1:13), as foretold in Psalm 47:5 and 68:18. The disciples, overcome by this glorious event, bowed to the earth in worship, adoring Jesus as God (Matthew 28:9). Christians have celebrated Ascension Day as a special Church holiday since the third century. We especially anticipate His return.

9780758607140.